The Biblical Doctrine of Virginity

The
Biblical Doctrine
of Virginity

Lucien Legrand M.E.P.

SHEED & WARD - NEW YORK

First Published 1963

Nihil obstat: J. Alazard, M.E.P., Censor deputatus,
die 21a januarii, 1963
Nihil obstat: Bernadus Can. Patten, S.T.D., S.S.L., *Cens. Lib.*
Imprimatur: Dionysius McDonnell, *Vic. Gen.*
Liverpolii, die 13a Aprilis 1963
Library of Congress Catalog Card No. 63-17413

Contents

List of Abbreviations vii

Foreword *by Thomas Worden* ix

Preface xiii

Introduction 19

I The Prophetical Value of Virginity

Chapter One The Prophecy of the Final Doom 25

   1. The celibacy of Jeremias 25

   2. 'On account of the present necessity' 30

Chapter Two Virginity and the Kingdom 37

II The Sacrificial Value of Virginity

Chapter Three Virginity and the Cross 53

   1. Teaching on celibacy 53

   2. A daily cross 61

Chapter Four Virginity as an Apotheosis 71

   1. Continence and cult in the Old Testament 72

   2. Virginity and the cult of the New Testament 78

III The Spiritual Value of Virginity

Chapter Five Virginity and Liberty 89

Chapter Six Virginity and Charity 101

Chapter Seven   Virginal Fecundity   113
        1. The Spirit   114
        2. The Virgin   121
        3. Fecundity according to the Spirit   125
        4. Spiritual fecundity in the Church   134
        Conclusion   141

Conclusion   147

General Index   155

Index of Scripture References   161

Index of Greek Words   167

List of Abbreviations

AAS	*Acta Apostolicae Sedis* (Rome, 1908)
BJ	*La Sainte Bible traduite en français sous la direction de l'Ecole Biblique de Jérusalem*
ERE	*Encyclopedia of Religions and Ethics* (ed. J. Hastings)
ICC	*International Critical Commentary*
NTS	*New Testament Studies* (Cambridge, 1954)
PG	*Patrologiae Cursus Completus. Series Graeca* (ed. Migne)
PL	*Patrologiae Cursus Completus. Series Latina* (ed. Migne)
RB	*Revue Biblique* (Paris, 1892)
SDBV	*Supplément. Dictionnaire de la Bible* (ed. L. Pirot, A. Robert, H. Cazelles)
Str.-Bil.	H. L. Strack-P. Billerbeck: *Kommentar zum Neuen Testament aus Talmud und Midrasch*[2], (Munich, 1956)
Text. Rab.	J. Bonsirven: *Textes Rabbiniques des deux premiers Siècles Chrétiens pour servir à l'intelligence du Nouveau Testament* (Rome, 1955)
TWNT	*Theologisches Wörterbuch zum Neuen Testament* (ed. G. Kittel)

Foreword

THE PRACTICE of celibacy has always aroused the curiosity of the world at large, and never more so than in our own day. It is a practice which has often provoked feelings either of admiration or revulsion, but rarely been properly understood. And it must be admitted that help towards a proper understanding of celibacy is not easy to find. For the most part it has come from apologists, who have felt compelled to refute the common objections that celibacy is an unnatural state, productive of grave psychological disturbances, and symptomatic of a self-centredness which is anti-social. In reply to such misunderstandings it has frequently been pointed out that celibacy does in certain circumstances enable a man to devote himself more single-mindedly to the development of his particular talents, and that far from being a selfish egotist the celibate has chosen to renounce a deeply treasured right to marriage in order to devote himself the more to the welfare of his fellow men.

A defence of celibacy on these lines is eminently reasonable. But it is both misleading and insufficient, because the only celibacy which has had its apologists is Christian celibacy, and Christian celibacy is not to be properly understood through a demonstration of its reasonableness. To show that

Christian celibacy is not contrary to right reason is insufficient. Neither is it enough to show its so-called practical advantages. Indeed it is open to question whether the latter outweigh its practical disadvantages. But there can be no doubt that to explain Christian celibacy first and foremost in terms of what is reasonable and useful is inevitably to fail to give a true understanding. In presenting the Christian view of sex in all its aspects we have often appeared as enlightened humanists rather than believers in a higher wisdom which is God's revelation in Christ. The aim has been a laudable one, namely to instruct and influence those who are not Christians. But the price we have paid for a dubious success has been too high, because the Christian ideal has become obscure to Christians themselves.

To dissipate this obscurity Fr Legrand illuminates Christian celibacy in the light of Christ's death and resurrection. The Christian seeks to explain himself to the world in the same way as St Paul: 'For what we preach is not ourselves, but Jesus Christ as Lord, with ourselves as your servants for Jesus' sake. For it is the God who said, "Let light shine out of darkness," who has shone in our hearts to give the light of the knowledge of the glory of God in the face of Christ.' (II Cor 4:5-6). The face of Christ shown to the world is the appearance of him who died and who rose from the dead. As Christians we must share in his death and resurrection. As witnesses of Christ we must proclaim his death and resurrection. No action nor state of life is Christian unless it does this. And among the diversity of gifts offered to us by the Holy Spirit, none is more suited to the proclaiming of Christ's death and resurrection than that gift of the Spirit which is Christian celibacy. This book shows us how celibacy is indeed a prophecy or proclamation that the kingdom of God is at hand; that Christ has died and risen again for our salvation, and that out of death has sprung forth new life.

It is the great and the rare merit of this book that it shows celibacy to be one of the brightest facets of the Church, as she fulfils her destiny of reflecting the light of Christ to the world.

T. Worden

Upholland College,
Wigan, Lancs.

Preface

APART FROM a few alterations, the studies which make up this book have already appeared in various reviews. The first four chapters were originally published in *Scripture* (XII, 1960, pp. 97-105; XIII, 1961, pp. 12-20; XIV, 1962, pp. 1-12, 65-75); chs. 5 and 6 in *Indian Ecclesiastical Studies* (I, 1962, pp. 175-195) and ch. 7 in *Nouvelle Revue Théologique* (LXXXIV, 1962, pp. 785-805). I am deeply indebted to the editors of these reviews for kindly allowing me to reprint the papers in book form.

I am especially grateful to the Rev. T. Worden, S.T.L., L.S.S., the editor of *Scripture*. This work owes much to him. But for his encouragement and suggestions, it is unlikely that this study would ever have gone further than the few observations on Jeremias and St Paul which constitute the first chapter. It takes some boldness to think of writing and publishing, when one lives some 5000 miles away from the great centres of biblical learning. I owe it to the Rev. T. Worden that I overcame my initial shyness and attempted to work upon what were originally unformed impressions rather than real ideas. Moreover he agreed to read through and to amend the manuscript. I want to express my whole-hearted gratitude to him.

Though the book consists of papers initially published separately, I trust that the reader will find in it more than a vague collection of studies loosely grouped round a common theme. There runs through these pages a plan which unfolded itself spontaneously in the actual course of my reflexions.

Like any Christian reality, virginity has a triple reference to the past, the present and the future, because it shows forth eminently the condition of the faithful in the present period of salvation. Anchored in the sacrifice of Christ, it announces the advent of the world to come, which it already anticipates. It is thus at the same time commemoration, promise and fulfilment. In a way we can apply to virginity what the Liturgy says of the Holy Eucharist: it recalls the sacrifice of the Lord, is a gift of divine grace and a pledge of the life to come.

And because the Christian fact has a double aspect of death and life, because the sacrifice of Christ was immolation and consecration, because the age to come brings with it fullness of life through death, because Christian life is made up of renunciation and love, it follows that each of the three angles from which virginity can be surveyed had to be taken successively in a negative and in a positive way. Hence the six chapters of this work, to which was added, by way of conclusion and synthesis, a study on the virginal fecundity of Mary and of the Church.

At the outset of this study, a word should be said on the matter of vocabulary. Ought we to speak of virginity, celibacy, perfect chastity or continence? Each term has overtones of its own. Continence is rather negative, mainly denoting abstinence from the use of matrimony. It would apply well to the Buddhist ideal of renunciation; it is insufficient to express the attitude of loving dedication which must animate Christian 'continence'. Celibacy would be rather too broad: it refers to a social condition which may have no religious bearing at all. One may remain a celibate out of selfishness or because of circumstances. Christian 'celibacy', to have any Christian value, must be dedicated and willingly accepted; otherwise it is lifeless. Virginity is a traditional term in the Catholic Church. But it has a feminine ring. In spite of the attempts of spiritual authors, its use in the masculine remains strained and clumsy. Moreover, of itself, it lays the stress on a physical integrity which has little to do with the viewpoint of the New Testament. The theology sketched here is not properly speaking a theology of virginity since it could apply as well to widows and penitents. Finally, 'perfect chastity', which is also traditional, might be rather misleading since it could wrongly convey the impression that married life is 'imperfect', cannot be really 'chaste', and bears some kind of original stain.

Actually, on the point we are concerned with, we notice a fact which the theologian faces in all his fields of study: words are unable by themselves to account for Christian realities. It is only Christian usage and tradition which makes them equal to the message they have to convey.

We have made use of the different terms somewhat freely, with no other guide than their suitability in the given context. What matters is the context and the realities which words imperfectly describe. The authors of the New Testament themselves have not discriminated in their use of the vocabulary. They speak of παρθένος, ἄγαμος, ἐγκρατής. And did not Jesus use the word 'eunuch' to describe the Christian virgins? Theology has to do violence to linguistic purism as the Kingdom does violence to nature.

In his inspiring study on celibacy,[1] M. Thurian shuns the word virginity because he suspects it of bearing traces of a half-Pelagian and half-Manichean superiority complex, implying contempt for marriage. Behind that kind of sensitiveness to a word which has long been traditional in the Church, there may still loom the old problem of the value of good works, which has divided Catholics and Protestants from the beginning. Is it not possible to remain a virgin without a superiority complex and to do good without pride?

May we hope that this study will play its part in removing this misunderstanding and that it will prepare some common ground on which some may find the evangelical roots of a traditional practice, while others will be reminded of its predominantly theological and charismatic sources?

That it may be so is our humble prayer in laying the present work at the feet of the Virgin of Virgins whose virginity the Holy Spirit had prepared to be the human cradle of God's Word.

St Peter's Seminary,
Bangalore, India.
April, 1962.

---

[1] *Mariage et Célibat,* Neuchâtel-Paris, 1955.

Introduction

Introduction

A GOOD study of biblical theology usually begins with the Old Testament. For example the theologian may look in the Old Law for the first outlines of a doctrine of grace, of the Church, the Spirit and even of the Trinity.

It can hardly be so with a biblical study of virginity. For virginity is essentially a Christian institution.

The Old Testament, on the whole, does not acknowledge any religious value in virginity.

Thus, when Jephte's daughter realized that she had to die in fulfilment of her father's vow, she withdrew to the mountains 'to bewail her virginity' (Jg 11:37-40). It is significant that what she laments over is her virginity. For herself, her father, her companions and those who recorded that tradition, what made her fate so pitiful was not the fact that she had to leave the world in the bloom of her youth: this is a romantic view which does not belong to stern biblical times. For the Israelites the pathos of her story lies in the fact that she will not experience the joys of matrimony and motherhood. She will die a virgin, and this is a curse, a disgrace similar to the shame attached to sterility (cf Lk 1:25). The ancient East thought little of women and in that respect the Hebrews were no more chivalrous than their

19

neighbours. A woman was esteemed only as a mother, so that sometimes, by metonymy, she was called simply *raḥam*, a womb (Jg 5:30).[1] What Israel had regard for was mother-hood rather than womanhood as such. What was a virgin then but a girl, a female not yet married, still deprived of what was to give sense to her existence? Virginity, like sterility, was a deficiency, a reproach, a base condition: Mary will speak of the 'baseness' of her virginal condition (Lk 1:48).

The prophets had a similar thought in mind when, in their lamentations, they gave the chosen people the title of 'Virgin of Israel': 'Listen to my lamentation, house of Israel! . . . She has fallen, she shall not rise again, the Virgin of Israel.' In this text, Amos (5:2; cf Jl 1:8; Lam 1:15; 2:13), by calling Israel a virgin, wants to emphasize her misery: she will die like a virgin, without leaving any descendants. It is like an echo, on a collective level, of the laments of Jephte's daughter.

These examples show clearly that according to the old Semitic mentality virginity is far from being an ideal. It is fecund matrimony which is honourable and a sign of God's blessing (Ps 127:3-5). The same applies to men. L. Köhler remarks that the Hebrew of the Old Testament has no word for bachelor, so unusual is the idea.[2]

Towards the end of the Old Testament period, at least some groups among the Essenes observed celibacy, and their

[1] The same metonymy is also to be found on the Mesha stone, line 17. Cf J. Pedersen, *Israel, its Life and Culture*, I-II, London 1926, pp. 70, 508. There is also the saying of Rabbi Yuda: 'Every day we should say three blessings: Blessed is he who did not make me a pagan, a woman, an ignorant man . . .' (*Text. Rab.*, p. 116, no. 493. See, in the same work, texts no. 911, 1590).

[2] *The Hebrew Man*, London 1956, p. 89. The Rabbis said: 'A man who is not married is not truly a man' (*Yebamot* 63a).

influence may be felt in the life of John the Baptist.[1] Unfortunately the authors who mention this observance of the Essenes are very vague about its motives. Josephus (*De Bello Judaico* ii, 8, 2) and Philo (quoted by Eusebius: *Praep. ev.*, viii, 11. *PG* 21, 644 ab), putting themselves on the level of their pagan readers, reduce the celibacy of the Essenes to a misogyny entirely void of any religious value: 'They beware of the impudence of women and are convinced that none of them can keep their faith to a single man', says Josephus. Pliny (*Hist. nat.* v, 17) describes the Essenes as philosophers, 'tired of life' (*vita fessos*), who give up the pleasures of love: Essenian celibacy would be of a Stoical type, but obviously Pliny's competency may be doubted when it comes to interpreting the motives of a Hebrew sect. The Qumran texts might have given us an explanation, but so far they have not been very helpful on this question. Though they know of a temporary continence on the occasion of the eschatological war,[2] they do not impose celibacy on the members of the Community. On the contrary, the *Rule*

[1]Mary's vow of virginity, if we accept it, might be explained by a similar influence: see R. Laurentin, *Structure et Théologie de Luc I-II*, Paris 1957, pp. 183-187. We have omitted in this study to discuss the question of whether Mary had made such a vow before the Annunciation or not. The problem is not easy. Mary's answer to the angel in Lk 1:34 does not necessarily postulate a vow. On the other hand, Laurentin is right in insisting that there was at that time in Judaism a movement in favour of dedicated celibacy, which makes it less unlikely that a pious Hebrew girl would have decided to keep her virginity throughout her life. Anyway, in the framework of our study, the question may be left open. As will be shown later, what matters most in the case of the Virgin Mary is not the moral example she gave but the theological significance of her virginal motherhood in the history of salvation. And this significance does not depend on the existence or not of a vow of virginity prior to the Annunciation.

[2]'No toddling child or woman is to enter their camp from the moment they leave Jerusalem to go to war until they return . . .' (*The War of the Children of Light*, vii, 3-4).

21

Annexe speaks explicitly of women and children,[1] and the discovery of female skeletons in the cemetery of the Community[2] makes it clear that at Qumran as in the sect of Damascus[3]—if the two sects were distinct—matrimony was as least allowed. In short, a few groups among the Essenes present an interesting case of pre-Christian celibacy; its study might throw some light on the New Testament ideal of virginity, but such a study is handicapped by the lack of reliable explanation of their motives. And when we do come across first-hand contemporary documentation, it happens that this concerns a sect which did not observe celibacy as a rule.

It is only in the New Testament that a doctrine of celibacy can be found. There may here and there in the Old Testament be a few vague forebodings of the value of perfect chastity; but these do not go very far, and it is impossible to understand them unless they are seen in the context of the New Testament, where they are fulfilled. It is against the background of this context that the Old Testament antecedents of Christian celibacy will be studied—in particular, the case of Jeremias, especially interesting since it is the only clear case of voluntary celibacy among the figures of the Old Testament. But, as will be seen, this case remains purely negative: Jeremias did not consider his condition as the embodiment of an ideal, but as a fatal necessity. We must come to Jesus (Mt 19:12) and his disciples, Paul (I Cor 7) and Luke (Lk 1), to find virginity glorified and given a place of its own in the framework of biblical revelation.

[1]*Rule Annexe* i, 4, 9-10. See texts in A. Dupont-Sommer, *The Essene Writings from Qumran*, London 1961, pp. 104f with a footnote discussing the problem of Essene celibacy. This problem is also treated by G. Vermès, 'Quelques traditions de Qumran' in *Cahiers Sioniens* 9 (1955), pp. 42-44.
[2]Cf *RB* 63 (1956), pp. 569-572.
[3]*Document of Damascus* iv, 20 - v, 6; vii, 6-8.

I

The Prophetical Value of Virginity

CHAPTER ONE

The Prophecy of the Final Doom

1. The celibacy of Jeremias

IF WE have to come to the New Testament in order to find virginity extolled and put forward as an ideal, there is yet in the Old Testament a case of celibacy which is worth studying: it is that of Jeremias, 'a virgin prophet and a figure of the Great Prophet who was also a virgin and the son of a virgin'.[1]

Jeremias was apparently the first biblical character to embrace celibacy as a state of life. At least he is the first one to whom Scripture explicitly attributes celibacy. Others before him may have abstained from marriage. Ancient Christian writers often suppose that Elias did so[2] and make him the father of monastic life. But the testimony of the Bible concerning Elias is purely negative: no wife is mentioned, but the Bible does not speak of his celibacy either. Even if he remained a celibate, we have no indications as to his reasons. Jeremias, on the contrary, in his Confessions speaks of his celibacy and explains it. We may owe this insight into his private life to his introspective mood, another quality that was rare in ancient Israel. Anyway he pro-

---

[1]Bossuet, *Méditations sur l'Evangile*, cix[th] day.
[2]See texts in *Elie le Prophète* (*Etudes Carmélitaines* 1956) I, pp. 165, 189. But St Augustine was not convinced of the celibacy of Elias: cf *De Genesi ad litteram* ix, 6.

vides us with the earliest reflection on celibacy. In it we can trace to its beginnings the biblical doctrine of virginity.

> The word of the Lord came to me saying:
> Do not take a wife; have no sons and no daughters in this place. For thus says the Lord concerning the sons and daughters that are born here and concerning the mothers that bore them and concerning the fathers who begot them in this land:
> They shall die miserably, without being lamented, without being buried.
> They shall be as dung upon the face of the earth.
> They shall perish by the sword and by famine.
> Their carcasses shall be a prey for the birds of the air and the wild animals.
>
> (Jer 16:1-4)

Those are the terms in which Jeremias explains his celibacy. Are these verses to be understood as a positive order of God, given to the prophet when he came of age and enjoining him to abstain from matrimony? It might be said that celibacy was progressively imposed upon the prophet by the circumstances, his isolation and the persecutions that made him an outcast. Eventually he would have understood that beneath those circumstances there was a divine ordinance and, with typical Hebrew disregard for secondary causes, he would have expressed it in the literary form of an order. In any case, it is clear that Jeremias gives his celibacy a symbolic value. The loneliness of his unmarried life forebodes the desolation of Israel. Death is about to sweep over the country. Jeremias' forlorn celibacy is nothing but an enacted prophecy of the imminent doom. Calamity will be such as to render matrimony and procreation meaningless.

Jeremias' celibacy is to be understood as a prophecy in action. Symbolic actions were frequent among the prophets. Thus to announce the imminent captivity of the Egyptians, Isaias walks naked in the streets of Jerusalem (Is 20:1-6). Jeremias breaks a pot to symbolize the destruction of the capital (Jer 19:1-11). Ezechiel makes a plan of the siege to come, cooks impure food as the famished inhabitants of the besieged city will have to do, cuts his beard and scatters it to the four winds as the population of Juda will be scattered (Ez 4:1-5:4). In some cases it was the whole life of a prophet which was given a symbolical significance by God: for instance Osee's matrimonial misfortunes symbolized the un-happy relations between Yahweh and his unfaithful spouse Israel (Os 1-3).

Jeremias' life too was symbolic. He lived in times of distress. He was to be a witness of the destruction of Sion. It was his sad duty to announce the imminent desolation: 'Every time I have to utter the word, I must shout and proclaim: Violence and ruins!' (Jer 20:8). Still more: it was his tragic destiny to anticipate in his existence and signify by his own life the terrible fate of the 'Virgin of Israel'.

'The Virgin of Israel' was soon to undergo the fate of Jephte's daughter, to die childless, to disappear without hope. With his prophetic insight, Jeremias could see already the shadow of death spreading over the country. He could hear already the moaning of the land:

> Teach your daughter this lamentation:
> Death has climbed in at our windows;
> she has entered our palaces,
> destroyed the children in the street,
> the young men in the square.
> Corpses lie like dung all over the country. (Jer 9:19-21)

27

This was no mere Oriental exaggeration. What Israel was about to witness and Jeremias had to announce was really the death of Israel. Israel had been living by the Covenant and now, by the sin of the people, the Covenant had been broken. The two institutions in which the Covenant was embodied and through which God's graces came down upon the people, the two great signs of God's indwelling in the land of his choice, the Temple and kingship, would soon disappear. Only a few years more and Nabuchodonosor would invade Juda, burn the sanctuary, enslave the king and kill his children. For the Israelites this would be the end of a world, the day of the Lord, day of doom and darkness, day of return to the original chaos (Jer 4:23-31; 15:2-4). Ezechiel will explain in a dramatic way the meaning of the fall of Jerusalem: the Glory of God will leave his defiled abode and abandon the land (Ez 8:1-11:25). Israel will die and nothing short of a resurrection will bring her to life (Ez 37:1-14). When the exiles leave Palestine, Rachel can sing her dirge at Rama (Jer 31:15): her children are no more. Israel as a people has disappeared. God's people have been dispersed. There are no more heirs of the promises and children of the Covenant unless God repeats the Exodus and creates a new people. A Testament is over. God's plan has apparently failed. Death reigns.

Prophetically Jeremias sees all that beforehand. He experiences it proleptically in his flesh. Excluded from the temple (Jer 36:5), excommunicated so to say from his village (Jer 12:6; 11:19-23) and from the community (Jer 20:2; 36:26), he, before the exile, will experience what it means to live estranged from one's country, away from the temple of the Lord. Before the Israelites, he knows the bitter taste of a life which has no hope left on earth. 'Never could I sit joyful

28

in the company of those who were happy; forlorn I was under the power of thy hand for thou hadst filled me with wrath' (Jer 15:17).

Thus was Jeremias' life an anticipation of the imminent doom. So was his celibacy. When Death already casts her shadow over the land, is it a time to marry? 'For thus says Yahweh Sabaoth, the God of Israel: Behold I will put an end, in this place, under your very eyes and in your very days, to the shouts of gladness and of mirth, to the songs of the bride and of the bridegroom' (Jer 16:9). An end of joy, life, marriage: the country turns into a sheol: there is no marriage and no begetting in the sheol. The command of the Lord to 'increase and multiply' (Gen 1:28) assumed that the world was good (Gen 1:4, 10, etc.). But now that man's sin has roused death, the Lord reverses his command: 'Do not take a wife; have no sons and no daughters in this place.' Jeremias' life of solitude announces the reign of death and anticipates the end of the world he lived in. His celibacy is in line with his message of doom. It is part of those trials by which 'the most suffering of the prophets', as St Isidorus of Pelusia puts it,[1] anticipates God's judgment. It is part of the sufferings which point to the cross, the final expression of God's judgment. The solitude of the lonely prophet of Anatoth announces the dereliction of the crucified victim of Calvary. It has the same significance: it signifies the end of an economy in which God's promises and graces were entrusted to Israel *secundum carnem* and communicated by way of generation. This order disappears. When God will raise a new Israel, it will be an Israel *secundum spiritum* in which one will have access not by right of birth but by direct recep-

---

[1] 'τῶν προφητῶν πολυπαθέστατος', *PG* 78, 356.

tion of the Spirit (Jer 31:31-35). In such a people the fecundity of the flesh will have lost its value.

2. 'On account of the present necessity'

Replying to a question of the Corinthians concerning virgins, St Paul's advice is to leave them in that state. But the explanation he gives is not very clear. 'I consider that it is better to be so on account of the present necessity' (I Cor 7:26). What is that 'present necessity' (ἐνεστῶσα ἀνάγκη) that justifies celibacy?

Catholic commentators (Cornely, Lemonnier, Allo, Callan, W. Rees, Osty, etc.) see in that 'necessity', as Osty puts it, 'the thousand worries of married life',[1] or else the imminent persecutions 'which an unmarried person is better able to bear'.[2] St Paul's position would be based on purely individual, psychological or ascetic grounds. On him who is married the burden of the world is more heavy. The celibate, on the contrary, can devote himself fully to the service of God.

Such a thought is certainly not foreign to St Paul's mind: he expresses it in vv. 32-35 of the same chapter.[3] Yet this does not seem to be his primary consideration. The immediate explanation he gives of his preference for celibacy follows another line: 'The time is short . . . The world in its present form is passing away' (vv. 29-31). This shows that his outlook is mainly collective and eschatological: the end of the world is drawing near: let us adapt our attitude to these new circumstances; it is time to detach ourselves from a doomed world. 'Even those who have a wife, let them live as if they

[1] *Epîtres aux Corinthiens* (*BJ*), Paris 1949, p. 40.
[2] W. Rees in *A Catholic Commentary on Holy Scripture*, Edinburgh 1953, p. 1090.
[3] See Ch 5, pp. 97-100 below.

had none . . . and those who have to deal with the world as if they had not.' Individual considerations are only an application of this view on the divine economy. It is because the times we are living in are the times of the end that it is better not to be burdened with matrimonial obligations, so as to be able to give one's undivided attention to God.

The vocabulary used by St Paul in this section confirms this eschatological interpretation of his views on celibacy. The words he uses clearly belong to the vocabulary of apocalyptic literature. The 'necessity' (ἀνάγκη) was the technical term used to describe the crisis of the last times (Lk 21:23; I Thess 3:7; Ps. Sal. 5:8; Test. Jos. 2:4); in that sense it is akin to 'tribulation' (θλῖψις) used here also to describe the present condition (v. 28) and which has also an apocalyptic value (Mt 24:9-28; Apoc 1:9; 7:14; II Thess 1:6). Similarly the term used for 'time' in v. 29 (καιρός) 'is about a technical term for the period before the Advent'[1] (cf Rom 13:11; Heb 9:9; I Pet 1:5, 11). It is true that these terms are not always taken in their technical eschatological sense. But their convergence and the context make it clear that St Paul sets virginity against an eschatological background. With Jeremias, he considers celibacy as a testimony that the last times have come, an attitude that presages the end.

The difficulty of this interpretation—and what makes Catholic commentators shrink from it—is that it seems to suppose in St Paul the erroneous belief that the end of the world was imminent. Can we accept such an explanation of celibacy without rallying to the 'consequent eschatology' of A. Schweitzer?[2]

[1] A. Robertson-A. Plummer: 'I Epistle of St Paul to the Corinthians' (*ICC*), Edinburgh 1911, p. 152.
[2] See the decree of the Biblical Commission of 18 June 1915 in *Enchiridion Biblicum*, 419-421.

Prat, followed by Huby and C. Spicq does not think the objection decisive. He accepts as possible, the eschatological explanation of virginity. Quoting I Cor 7:26-31, he comments: 'Is it possible that Paul was haunted by the near prospect of the Parousia? We must not deny this a priori ... Lacking certain knowledge, he might have formed an opinion based upon probabilities and conjectures ... It is at least possible that he guided his conduct and his counsels by such probabilities.'[1] This interpretation can be defended, provided we attribute to Paul not a positive teaching concerning the imminence of an event, the day and the hour of which none can know, but an opinion, a desire, a hope without certitude.[2] This is surely sufficient to safeguard biblical inerrancy and remain within the limits fixed by the Biblical Commission. Yet this exegesis is not fully satisfactory, for it leaves the impression that the eschatological explanation of celibacy should not be taken too seriously. It would be one of those views that reflect more the prejudices of the time than the Apostle's personal thought, like the arguments by which Paul tries to justify the imposition of the veil on women in the assembly (I Cor 11:2-16) or the midrashic allusion to the rock following the Jews in the desert (I Cor 10:4). Thus St Paul would have used the naive expectation of an imminent Parousia to insist on virginity, but that would be a mere *argumentum ad hominem* that should not be pressed too far. The real and solid ground for celibacy would remain the

[1] *Theology of St Paul*, I, London 1926, p. 112. Prat explained his mind still more clearly in a few pages of his final chapter on 'The Last Things' which he suppressed to satisfy an over-zealous censor. These pages have been published in Prat's biography by J. Calès: *Le Père Ferdinand Prat*, Paris 1942, pp. 99f.

[2] Cf J. Huby, *Première Epître aux Corinthiens* (*Verbum Salutis*), Paris 1946, p. 172. W. Rees also (*loc. cit.*) accepts an eschatological influence on St Paul's thought on virginity.

personal and ascetical considerations sketched in vv. 32-34.

Accepting Prat's eschatological interpretation of Paul's arguments for virginity, it may be possible to go deeper by comparing the thought of the Apostle with that of Jeremias. Is not the 'present necessity' of I Cor 7:26 parallel with the explanation Jeremias gave of his celibacy? If so, can we not find in Paul's eschatological justification of virginity a lasting value, something much deeper than a pious delusion?

It all amounts to a proper evaluation of his eschatological hope. Was it an illusion which he had, but which he avoided expressing firmly? Or was it on the contrary a central element of his faith and of his spiritual outlook? O. Cullmann, for the early Church in general,[1] and L. Cerfaux, for St Paul in particular,[2] have shown that it is the second view which is true. There is much more than a question of knowing whether Paul or the early Church did or did not expect an imminent Parousia. For them and for us the heart of the matter is not the date of the Parousia but its significance. What is the impact of the Parousia on our present life? In Cullmann's terms, what is the connection of the present period of history (the times of the Church) with the past (death and resurrection of Christ) and the future (final resurrection)?[3] The problem is not chronological but theological. St Paul may or may not have been under the impression that Christ was soon to return. This is rather immaterial and irrelevant. What matters is that, for him, and for the early Christians, ours are the last days (Ac 2:16ff). The last hour has begun with the death of the Lord (I Jn 2:18). How long will it be? Nobody knows, but it is clear that now, in Christ, history has

[1] See particularly *Le Retour du Christ*, Neuchâtel, 1945.
[2] *Christ in the Theology of St Paul*, Edinburgh 1958, pp. 62-71.
[3] Cf O. Cullmann, *Christ et le Temps*, Neuchâtel 1947, pp. 102-123.

3

reached its end, and what we witness now in the world is the consummation of the end: 'The world goes on disappearing' (I Jn 2:17). The Apocalypses of St John and of the synoptic Gospels show in veiled language that the trials the Church has to undergo are the forerunning signs of the consummation, and St Paul explains that the individual tribulations of Christians are their share of the Messianic woes (Col 1:24).[1]

The present period may be short or long; after all, 'with the Lord, one day is as thousand years and a thousand years as one day' (2 Pet 3:8). In any case Christian life is thoroughly eschatological in character. Whatever may be the actual date of the Parousia, we live after the end of history has been reached. We are just waiting for the consummation of the end, we turn towards it and we prepare it. The Parousia hangs, so to say, over our life: even if chronologically it may be still distant, theologically it is imminent: it is the only development of the history of salvation that we can expect, and it colours our outlook on things. Seen in the light of faith, the history we live in and our personal fate appear as signs of the end. Celibacy is one of those signs: it shows that the last times have come. It proclaims that the world is disappearing. The end has come. Man's primary duty is no more to continue the human species. It is on the contrary to free himself from a fleeting world which has already lost its substance. This is not an attitude of panic before a threatening disaster. It is rather an act of faith in the significance of the Lord's death, the beginning of the end.

---

[1] In Col 1:24, θλῖψις τοῦ Χριστοῦ should be translated 'the messianic woes' and not the 'sufferings of Christ' (θλῖψις is not πάθημα). The phrase does not refer to the sufferings of our Lord, but, according to terminology common in Judaism, to the trials God's people had to undergo to reach the messianic times, the birth-pangs of the new world.

Thus Paul understood virginity exactly as Jeremias did. Jeremias did not know the date of the destruction of Jerusalem: it is not the role nor the charisma of the prophets to give a chronology of the future. But one thing he knew for certain: on account of the infidelity of the people the former Covenant had become void. Consequently the old institutions like the Temple and kingship would break like empty shells and Israel, abandoned by God, would collapse. He knew that his was a time of death. The nuptial songs would be replaced by lamentations. Marriage and procreation had lost their meaning. The prophet showed it by his own life: his celibacy was an enacted lamentation.

Similarly, St Paul did not know the date of the end. But he knew for certain that the world had condemned itself by condemning Christ and that the worldly powers had been nailed down on the Cross. It was God's plan to leave some interval before the actual end of all, time to allow the mystery of iniquity to reach its climax and the Church to spread all over the world. During that time life was to continue and marriage was still legitimate. Yet even married people had to understand that they were no longer of the world they were in. Still using this world, they had to be detached from it. Even to marriage they had to bring an attitude of freedom, a tension towards a higher form of love, the love of Christ towards his bride the Church (cf Eph 5:25-33). And it is quite fitting that to remind men of the objectivity they should keep towards a fleeting world, there should be in the Church a special charisma (I Cor 7:7) of virginity, akin to the charisma of prophecy. The celibate's life is an enacted prophecy. His whole life shouts to the world that it is passing away. As Jeremias announced to the chosen people the end of the Old Covenant, so the celibate,

35

a new Jeremias, announces the end of the old world. He embodies the teachings of the Apocalypses. He stands as a witness of the Day of the Lord, the Day of Wrath and of Death which began on that Friday of Nisan when the Lamb was slaughtered on Mount Calvary.

CHAPTER TWO

Virginity and the Kingdom

THE LAST days are not only days of doom: they are also days of resurrection. Jeremias was not only the prophet of the fall of Jerusalem: he was also the prophet of the New Covenant (Jer 31:31-35). Similarly for St Paul the last days are only secondarily days of woe: primarily, they are the days of the Parousia when Christ will come and hand over to the Father the world revivified by the Spirit (I Cor 15). The Apocalypse ends its enumeration of the eschatological calamities by the resplendent description of the heavenly Jerusalem where everything is made new (Apoc 21). Christ's death on Calvary was only the beginning of his Exaltation (Jn 3:14f; 12:32f). The full prophetical meaning of virginity is to be understood in reference to the whole mystery of death and life contained in Christ. Celibacy is not only an enacted prophecy of imminent doom: it announces also and anticipates the life to come, the life of the new world in the Spirit.

Jeremias, who had announced the New Covenant, might have understood that virginity would be the typical state in that new life which was no longer to be granted by the power of the flesh but by the Spirit. But in fact he does not seem to have realized these implications of his prophetical teaching. Or, if he did, he had no occasion to express his realization. We have to come to the Gospels to find this doctrine expounded.

Jesus lived a celibate life. Yet there is very little in the Gospels about virginity. This is not surprising. The Gospels are only factual summaries. There is little room in them for introspection and self-analysis. They have little to say about Jesus' personal life. They do not tell us how he felt when praying, when working miracles, when undergoing the trials of his Passion. It is no wonder therefore that they should be almost completely silent concerning Jesus' celibacy. This silence gives more value to the one statement in the Gospels in which Christ explained how he understood his virginity.

It was on an occasion in which he had emphasized once more the law of the indissolubility of matrimony. The disciples could hardly understand the intransigence of the Master. As usual Jesus tried to bring light to the discussion by taking it to a higher level. The heart of the matter is not the convenience of men but the requirements of the King- dom of God. The Kingdom of God does make exacting demands upon its members. See the case of those to whom it has been given to realize fully the implications of the coming of the Kingdom: they can be compared to eunuchs!

> There are eunuchs who were born so from their mother's womb and there are eunuchs who were made so by men and there are eunuchs who have made them- selves so in view of the Kingdom of Heaven. (Mt 19:12)

Though this pericope appears in Mt only, there is no reason to deny its authenticity. In his book on the synoptic Gospels, L. Vaganay insists several times that Mt 19:10-12, along with several other passages, though appearing in one Gospel only, belongs to the oldest layer of the Gospel formation, and to the most ancient tradition common to the three synoptic Gospels.[1] If the text figures in Mt only, it is not because it was added afterwards to the final edition of the book: it is not a case of addition by Matthew but of omission by Mark and Luke. The pericope on the eunuchs has an archaic ring that would have been shocking to Gentile ears. It is the kind of coarse Semitic paradox, frequent in the Bible, quite appealing to the rough peasant of Palestine, accustomed to the loud and often brutal eloquence of the prophets. It could hardly be exported to Greece or even to Asia Minor or Egypt. It is not surprising that Mark and Luke preferred to drop it. Yet 'its very paradoxical aspect guarantees its authenticity'.[2]

Moreover, the parallel text of Mk seems to leave traces of the amputation. In Mk 10:10, after the discussion with the Pharisees on matrimony, Jesus returns home together with his disciples. There is a change of place and of audience: Jesus is now in the intimate circle of his disciples. Usually, when he retires together with them, it is to teach a deeper doctrine (Mk 4:10, 34; 7:17; 9:30; 10:32). One would expect here, 'at home', further explanations on the views he has just exposed. Yet, according to Mk 10:10-12, Jesus merely repeats the elementary explanations which, according to Mt 19:9; 5:32 and Lk 16:18, he would give to the crowds as well. Does not this mean that in the sources Mark used, there was 'at home' some other deeper teaching imparted to the disciples? And what other teaching was there except the logion on the eunuchs recorded by Mt? Mark removed that saying, but the operation has left a scar in the text.

[1] L. Vaganay, *Le Problème Synoptique*, Paris-Tournai 1954, pp. 167, 211, 216, etc.
[2] *Ibid.*, p. 167.

If the pericope does belong to the origins of the Gospel composition, there is no reason to doubt that it was really an utterance of Jesus, and this decides the question of its bearing.

In the concrete context of Jesus' celibate life, it is easy to find out to whom the third category of eunuchs refers. When the disciples heard that saying, they could only think of Jesus himself and possibly also of John the Baptist. It is clear that Jesus here speaks of his own case and explains it. He does not advocate self-mutilation: he sets up his own example. He observed virginity and he did so consciously 'in view of God's Kingdom'. John the Baptist had done so before him; others would follow. Thus Jesus presents himself as the leader in a line of men who, thinking of God's Kingdom, will live like eunuchs, giving up the use of their sexual powers.[1]

But what exactly is the relationship between virginity and God's Kingdom? Why should one remain a celibate διὰ τὴν

[1] This evidently settles the problem, discussed from the time of Origen onwards, of whether the saying should be understood in a realistic or in a symbolic sense. In *TWNT* I, p. 590, K. L. Schmidt favours the realistic interpretation: the saying would allude to people who actually castrated themselves; it would invite the disciples not to imitate them but at least to reflect on their earnestness. Origen himself is a proof that there were such cases in the early Church. But was this so during Jesus' own lifetime? It is rather doubtful, and still more doubtful that Jesus would have set up as an example this hypothetic aberrant behaviour. Also in *TWNT* (II, p. 765), J. Schneider maintains the traditional interpretation.

The problem could be viewed also from the angle of Form Criticism. What were the concrete circumstances in the life of the early Church which led to these words of the Master being recalled? To what concrete problem were they given as an answer? It was most evidently the problem of the virgins, an acute problem as we know from I Cor 7 and possibly also, together with it, the problem of the widows 'who are truly widows' (I Tim 5:3-5; cf I Cor 7:8). According to J. Dupont, (*Mariage et Divorce dans l'Évangile*, Bruges 1959, pp. 218ff) the saying would refer to the case of husbands separated from their wives. This is a rather far-fetched *Sitz im Leben;* moreover it overlooks completely the reference to Jesus' own example.

βασιλείαν τῶν οὐρανῶν? What is the precise value of that διά? In Biblical Greek, διά with the accusative denotes causality or finality (out of, for the sake of, in view of). It is obvious that, in this context, the meaning must be of finality. But this is still very vague, too vague to use as the basis of an explanation of virginity. We cannot build a theology on the strength of a preposition.

If the preposition is vague, the phrase 'Kingdom of Heaven', on the contrary, is clear enough. The Kingdom of Heaven—or the Kingdom of God, since both phrases have the same significance[1]—appears as a key concept of the synoptic Gospels. It stands at the centre of Jesus' preaching. In Jesus' mouth, if not exactly in Judaism itself, it is 'a comprehensive term for the blessings of salvation',[2] having practically the same meaning as 'the age to come' or 'the life of the age to come'.[3] It is essentially an eschatological entity. What the Jews had longed for, the prophets had promised and the Apocalyptic writers had described, the new life coming from above, the new world, the new Covenant imparted by God, the new Israel, the gift of the Spirit, resurrection and re-creation: it is all that which is contained in God's Kingdom.

But—and this is the novelty of Jesus' teaching—with his coming, the eschatological world, the world to come, has become present, though it remains unfulfilled. With the coming of Jesus the Kingdom of God offers the paradoxical

---

[1]'The Heaven' is a term used by the Jews as a substitute for God, to avoid pronouncing the divine name.

[2]G. Dalman, *The Words of Jesus*, Edinburgh 1902, p. 135. Dalman shows that Jesus somewhat altered the meaning of the phrase by giving it a specifically eschatological value in connection with Dan 7:27. So, though in Judaism the phrase should be translated 'the kingship of God', it becomes, in Jesus' teachings, synonymous with eschatological salvation.

[3]Hence the equivalence with the Johannine theme of 'eternal life'.

character of being at the same time future and present. Jesus assures us that it is already present among us (Mt 12:28; cf Lk 17:21) but he also invites us to pray for its coming (Mt 6:10). Exegetes have tried to rationalize this mystery by reducing Jesus' preaching to one aspect or the other. The 'consequent eschatology' of A. Schweitzer retained only the future aspect: the life of Jesus was mere expectation which was deceived by the event. On the contrary, the 'realized eschatology' of C. H. Dodd retains only the present element: with Jesus, the Kingdom is present and there is nothing to expect from the future; eschatological elements should be dismissed as mere apocalyptic phraseology. Both views are only partial. W. G. Kümmel[1] and O. Cullmann,[2] among others, have shown that the integral teaching of Jesus combined both aspects. In Jesus the powers of the coming aeon are already active and the future Kingdom of God is already at work in the present. The divine Power is at work. Yet it works only like a seed: present in Jesus and in those who will follow him, it has still to extend its influence to the whole world till its life-giving activity covers and transforms the whole creation. Such is the meaning of the 'parables of the Kingdom' (Mk 4 and parallels). We are still waiting for the end: the period we live in is at the same time 'promise and fulfilment'.

This is apparent especially in the 'signs' of the Kingdom. According to the biblical conception, a 'sign' is not a pure symbol, faint image of a distant reality. It is the reality itself in its initial manifestation. In the biblical sign the coming reality is already contained, yet still hidden.[3] Kümmel has

[1]*Promise and Fulfilment*, London 1957.
[2]*Christ et le Temps*, Neuchâtel-Paris 1947.
[3]Cf J. Pedersen, *Israel, its Life and Culture*, I-II, 1926, pp. 168ff.

shown how in that sense Jesus' victory over the devils and his miracles are signs of that kind.[1] They show already 'the coming consummation of salvation breaking in on the present'.[2] Cullmann has added to those signs the main ecclesiastical functions: the missionary preaching of the Gospel,[3] the cult and the sacraments, for in them also, in the Spirit, and 'through the merits of Christ, everything is fulfilled which was accomplished in the past history of salvation and which will be achieved in the future'.[4]

In the light of Mt 19:12 we can add virginity to those signs. Like the miracles and the sacraments, virginity is a 'sign of the Kingdom', an anticipated realization of the final transformation, the glory of the world to come breaking in on the present condition. Such is the sense of Mt 19:12. Jesus and many of those who follow him refrain from sexual activity 'in view of the Kingdom', that is, to live already now the life of the world to come. Eschatological life has begun to stir in them and that life will be, and can now already be, a life which has gone beyond the necessity and the urge of procreation. As with their preaching and miracles, Jesus and his disciples by their virginity proclaim the advent of the Kingdom. They exemplify in this world the future condition of men in the next aeon.

This context reveals the meaning of the phrase διὰ τὴν βασιλείαν τῶν οὐρανῶν. It does not mean: 'in order to have access to the Kingdom': celibacy is not a necessary requirement to enter the Kingdom; it is a charismatic gift granted to a few only (v. 11). Neither should it be understood as 'to work more freely for the Kingdom': the text does not refer

[1]*Op. cit.*, pp. 105-121.
[2]*Ibid.*, p. 121.
[3]*Christ et le Temps*, pp. 111-117.
[4]O. Cullmann, *Early Christian Worship*, London 1953, p. 35.

to any particular work and the context does not concern preaching or carrying out a missionary apostolate. The proper paraphrase of 'in view of the Kingdom' would be: 'in order to be in harmony with the Kingdom'. The voluntary 'eunuchs' are so because they have found virginity to be the condition that corresponds best to the nature of the Kingdom.

As J. Dupont has pointed out,[1] there is an analogy between the three pericopes that follow each other in Mt 19:10-26. Chronologically they may belong to different periods of Jesus' ministry but they convey a similar lesson and it is for this purpose that Matthew has grouped them together. They reveal the nature of the Kingdom by showing forth its typical members. In the episode of the rich boy (Mt 19:16-26), the Kingdom appears as a kingdom of poverty (cf Mt 5:3). It is true that a place is left to the rich but it needs all the mighty grace of God to rescue them from their wealth and push them through the gate of the poor (v. 26; cf Lk 15; 16:1-9). Similarly the episode of the little children shows the Kingdom to be a kingdom of humility. Here again, those who are no longer children can obtain admittance but for that they have to be 'like unto them': the Kingdom belongs to those who have kept or recovered the simplicity and humility which is the spirit of childhood. The sayings on marriage and celibacy in vv. 3-12 have a similar bearing. The virgin's life is best adapted to the nature of the Kingdom: theirs is the Kingdom. Yet, here also, there is a place for those who are 'like unto them': married people can imitate the generosity of the voluntary 'eunuchs' and apply it to their conjugal life. But it is virginity that sets the pattern of the life to come: it is only by conforming his life with this pattern that man can be

[1] *Op. cit.*, pp. 202-207.

a member of the Kingdom. Even married life must be lived in the spirit which animates the virgins. It is only this spirit which may enable man and woman to face the exigencies of the divine matrimonial institution. The absolute indissolubility of wedlock and the unconditional ban on divorce belong to an order in which man is changed into a new being, the perfect image of which is given in virginity.

Jesus does not set impossible conditions on entry to the Kingdom. The rich, adults, wives and husbands are not barred from it. Yet it remains true that the Kingdom is a kingdom in which—as the parable of the workers in the next chapter will make clear—all worldly values are upset. The last become the first (19:30; 20:16) and the first the last; those whose condition places them on a level with the Kingdom are the poor, the children, the virgins. The poor are the typical citizens of the Kingdom for it is a kingdom which has other treasures than those of this world. Children have a right to it for it is a kingdom which knows another power than men rely upon. Finally the Kingdom belongs to virgins and to those like them, for it is a virginal kingdom, a kingdom that does not depend on the flesh for its life.

As Jesus explained to the Sadducees (Mt 22:30 and parallels), in the world of the Resurrection, 'one shall neither marry nor be married, one will be like the angels in heaven'. This does not mean that man in the Kingdom of God will be asexual, losing his human nature to become a pure spirit in the philosophical sense of the term. Such a philosophical consideration would be quite alien to the biblical mentality. Man was not made as a pure spirit either in this world or in the next, and consequently celibacy cannot consist in trying to ape the angels. St Luke explains the exact meaning of this analogy between risen man and the angels in his rendering

45

of the logion: 'They shall neither marry nor be married for they are no more liable to die: for they are equal to the angels and they are sons of God, being sons of Resurrection' (Lk 20:35f). The point of resemblance with the angels is not their spiritual nature but their immortality. It is on account of his immortality that the risen man need no longer procreate. The life of resurrection is no more a life 'in the flesh', a life doomed to death. It is a life in God, a life of the sons of God, life 'in the Spirit', in a body transformed by the divine glory. Hence the functions of the flesh become useless; procreation loses its meaning, which was to make up for the ravages of death.

The celibate shows by his condition that such a life has already started. His celibacy testifies to what O. Cullmann has called 'the proleptic deliverance of the body'.[1] It proclaims that, in Christ, despite appearances, man escapes the clutches of death and lives in the Spirit.

A passage of the Apocalypse echoes that teaching. Apoc 14:1-5 describes the glory of the Lamb in the heavenly Sion. There his throne is surrounded by a hundred and forty-four thousand men, all those who 'were redeemed from the earth'. They represent the perfect number of all those who, saved by the Lamb, will constitute his retinue in the world to come, namely all the elect. Their main characteristic consists in that 'they are virgins':

[1] O. Cullmann, *The Early Church*, London 1956, pp. 165-176. In his article, Cullmann does not extend his conclusions to the question of celibacy. He shows only that marriage has a special theological value since it 'corresponds to the relation between Christ and his Church' (p. 173; cf Eph 5:29). This view is quite true but should be complemented by an awareness that the love between Christ and the Church is of an eschatological—hence virginal—type. The Spouse is a Virgin (cf II Cor 11:2). Similarly, even conjugal love will have eventually to turn into the eschatological virginal *agapê* of which celibacy is a prophetical type. See ch 6, pp. 101-112 below.

In this passage, virginity must be understood meta-
phorically: it means primarily fidelity to God by opposition
to idolatry, often qualified in the Bible as a 'prostitution'.
Yet considering the realistic value of Hebrew symbolism,
the concrete sense of virginity should not be altogether
dismissed: 'they have not defiled themselves with women'
(v. 4).[1]

This passage must be understood in parallelism with
Apoc 7, which also describes a hundred and forty-four
thousand men leading an innumerable multitude which
surrounds the throne of the Lamb. Whilst in ch. 14 they
are all virgins, in ch. 7 they are all martyrs. This should not
be understood as meaning that only martyrdom can lead
to salvation. But it does mean that one has no access to the
Kingdom unless 'he washes his robe and makes himself
white in the blood of the Lamb' (Apoc 7:14). The martyr is
the typical Christian, for he shares most closely in the Cross
of his Master. One cannot be a Christian unless he shares in
some way in the fate of the martyrs, in the Cross of Christ.
The same interpretation can be extended to the fourteenth
chapter. 'As martyrdom, virginity is eminently representa-
tive of Christian life. Even as one cannot be saved without
participating in the dignity of martyrdom, one cannot be
saved without participating in the dignity of virginity.
Virginity is a heavenly perfection, an anticipation, for those
who are called to it, of what will be the final destiny of all in
the Kingdom of Heaven.'[2] In the world to come all are
virgins. Even those who are married must keep their eyes on
that ideal and know that their love has to turn into virginal

[1] Cf L. Cerfaux—J. Cambier, *L'Apocalypse de St Jean lue aux Chrétiens*, Paris
1955, pp. 124ff.
[2] L. Cerfaux—J. Cambier, *op. cit.*, p. 125.

charity. Those who remain celibate 'in view of the Kingdom of Heaven' belong to the virginal retinue of their heavenly King, the Lamb. As St Gregory of Nyssa says: 'Virginal life is an image of the happiness that will obtain in the world to come; for it contains in itself many signs of the good things which in hope are laid before us . . . For when one brings the life according to the flesh to an end in himself, as far as it depends on him, he can expect "the blessed hope and the coming of the great God", curtailing the interval of the intervening generations between himself and God's advent. Then he can enjoy in the present life the choicest of the good things afforded by the resurrection.'[1]

That is what Jesus exemplified in his life. His virginity inaugurated the new world where the flesh has no power, for that world knows no other life and no other fecundity than that of the Spirit. A later chapter will show that Mary's virginity had a similar meaning.[2]

So does the Christian's. It proclaims the disappearance of the world of flesh and the dawn of a new creation in the Spirit. The charisma of virginity in the Church has a prophetic value. The celibacy of Jeremias had prophesied the negative aspect of the mystery of the new Creation. To the Christian celibate it is given to know also its positive aspect, to live the fullness of the mystery and to announce it by his whole life. Like Jesus and Mary, the Christian celibate

---

[1] *De Virginitate*, *PG* 46, 381f. The words of St Cyprian also are well known: 'Quod futuri sumus, jam vos esse coepistis. Vos resurrectionis gloriam in isto saeculo jam tenetis; per saeculum sine saeculi contagione transitis' (*De habitu virginum* 22: *PL* 4, 462). The theme of celibacy as heavenly life is frequent in patristic literature: see L. Bouyer, *The Meaning of Monastic Life*, London 1955, pp. 23-40. Concerning the patristic doctrine of virginity, see the interesting booklet of Th. Camelot, *Virgines Christi, La Virginité aux Premiers Siècles de l'Eglise*, Paris 1944.
[2] Ch 7, pp. 114-121, below.

renounces worldly hope, for he knows that the world has no lasting hope to propose. But, at the same time, he announces and, through faith, already enjoys the eschatological visitation of the Spirit.

4

II

The Sacrificial Value of Virginity

Christian celibacy has a prophetic value: it foreshadows the new era. But it is a central point of the New Testament doctrine that the new era has already started with the sacrifice of Jesus. Christianity is wholly rooted in the central mystery of the death and resurrection of the Lord.

It must be the same with virginity if it is a genuine element of Christianity. Therefore we have now to turn from the future back to the past to find how virginity is anchored in the mystery of Calvary.

This search is not arbitrary. It was carried out by the first Christian generation: Paul and Luke will show us how it was done and with what results.

CHAPTER THREE

Virginity and the Cross

IN 14:26 and 18:29, St Luke adds 'a wife' to the list of the things which a disciple of Jesus must 'hate' or 'give up' to follow his Master. Those two small additions are worth considering: they open an interesting insight into the spirituality of St Luke and his understanding of Christian celibacy.

1. *Teaching on celibacy*

It is commonly granted that in both cases the 'wife' is an addition made by Luke.

In 18:29 this is almost obvious.[1] The parallel texts of Mt 19:29 and Mk 10:29 agree on an enumeration in which

[1] Mt 19:29	Mk 10:29f	Lk 18:29b-30
Everyone	There is no man	There is no man
that has left houses	that has left house	that has left house or wife
or brothers or sisters	or brothers or sisters	or brothers
or father or mother	or mother or father	or parents
or children or lands	or children or lands	or children
for my name's sake	for my sake and the sake of the Gospel	for the sake of God's Kingdom
shall receive	who shall not receive	who shall not receive
much more.	a hundred times as much.	much more.

53

family relations, grouped by pairs in quite a Semitic manner, were clumsily inserted between house and fields, without any reference to a wife.[1] As he was wont to do, Luke touched up his model delicately. Unlike Matthew, he did not try to correct the heaviness of the grammatical construction ('there is nobody that will . . . who shall not . . .'). But he improved the sentence by removing the 'lands', the reference to which came as an anticlimax at the end, and by simplifying the cumbersome Semitic enumeration. But mainly, and this was more than a stylistic correction, by adding 'wife', he completed the list of family bonds one has to cut in order to follow Christ.

Lk 14:26, a non-Markan passage, is another matter.[2] The parallel text in Mt 10:37 is so different that the first impression is that the two synoptists drew their material from various sources. Yet it should be noticed that in the following verse the two texts are much more closely connected. If a

---

[1] The list is so clumsy that quite a number of Mss of Mt, as well as Origen and Chrysostom, have corrected the text by shifting the 'lands' to the beginning of the enumeration. Other Mss (mostly those of the Antiochene family) added 'a wife' to the list of Mt. A lesser number added it also to Mk. It is the fairly common case of harmonization of the Synoptics. Merk has accepted the *Koinè* reading in his text of Mt (but not in Mk). The other manual editions are right in rejecting it.

[2]

Mt 10:37f	Lk 14:26f
He that loves father or mother	If somebody comes to me
more than me	and does not hate his father and
is not worthy of me	mother and wife and children
and he that loves son or daughter	and brothers and sisters
more than me	and even his own soul,
is not worthy of me	he cannot be my disciple.
and he that does not take his cross	Whoever does not carry his cross
and follow me	and come after me,
is not worthy of me.	he cannot be my disciple.

[3] Cf W. C. McAllen, *The Gospel according to St Matthew (ICC)*, Edinburgh 1912, p. 110; M.-J. Lagrange, *L'Evangile selon St Matthieu*, Paris 1948, p. 211.

common source is accepted for the latter, it must be accepted also for the former. In fact, the dissimilarity between the two texts of Matthew and Luke can easily be accounted for by a common source from which the two evangelists drew independently, both diverging from it in opposite directions.[1]

Technically, it must be Luke who reflects the source better: he keeps to the Semitic way of balancing in parallel elements of the enumeration; his simpler conclusion ('cannot be my disciple') is very likely to be closer to the original than the more sophisticated form of Matthew ('is not worthy of me'); the same can also surely be said of his typical semitism in the use of the verb μισεῖν (to hate) in the sense of not preferring.[2]

But there are indications that, though technically more faithful to his source, Luke also made his changes. In the original context, as it still stands in Matthew, the saying, a part of the missionary discourse, was a summary of Mic 7:6, quoted to illustrate the atmosphere of eschatological crisis in which the disciple must live: the last days have come when men must take up their position in the final struggle that will establish God's Kingdom; and the decision of the disciple may cut across his family loyalties and set him in opposition to his closest relatives. In Matthew and in Micheas, the wife was not mentioned among those relatives and it must have been the same in the source. Moreover the pair 'wife-children' in Luke breaks the perfect parallelism of the enumeration: a wife cannot be set in parallelism with children, as can father and mother or brothers and sisters. We may safely suppose therefore that, following Mic 7:6 and as the

[1] Cf L. Vaganay, *op. cit.*, p. 141.
[2] Cf R. Bultmann, *Die Geschichte der Synoptischen Tradition*, Göttingen 1957, p. 173.

text still stands in Matthew, the source must have had 'sons and daughters' after 'father and mother'. Luke substituted 'wife' for 'daughter' in order to introduce a favourite teaching of his. He made of the saying an invitation to total renounce- ment (cf. v. 33) suggesting that, to be perfect, the disciple should even forgo married life.

Commentators have noticed that it is typical of Luke to emphasize the requirements of the Gospel most strongly. Luke is an absolutist. 'All', 'none', 'everything' are favourite words of his vocabulary.[1] Renan spoke of Ebionitic ten- dencies in the third Gospel. As such, this statement is an anachronism but it can be said at least, with Lagrange, that Luke's Gospel is the 'Gospel of renouncement'.[2] Renouncing wife and children is, for Luke, one of the most significant forms of that radicalism in self-denial which he recom- mended.

But what exactly does Luke mean when he speaks of 'giving up' or 'hating' a wife? The fact that, in the two texts studied here, the word 'wife' was a deliberate addition of Luke shows that in both passages Luke's idea was the same. But what was that idea?

If the words were to be taken at their face value, it would seem, particularly in 18:29, that Luke envisages the case of a married man who abandons relatives, wife, children and belongings to devote himself to the service of God's Kingdom. The general trend of the sentence seems to impose that in- terpretation: exactly as one is assumed to have parents and properties and is invited to abandon them for the sake of the Kingdom, Luke would also take it for granted that one has a

[1] Cf J. Dupont, *Les Béatitudes*, Louvain 1954, p. 195. Dupont points to the same absolutism in 18:22; 5:11, 28; 12:33; Ac 2:44f; 4:32, 34f.
[2] *L'Evangile selon St Luc*, Paris 1948, p. xlv.

wife and children and should be advised to leave them, with the promise of a manifold reward. There is no doubt that the idea is strange. Exegetes do not usually consider the difficulty. Yet it does exist. Luke would practically advocate something akin to the Hindu *samnyâsana* ideal; Luke's suggestion would be similar to that of the Brahmanic books according to which, after a time of married life, when man has fulfilled his duty of procreation, he is advised to retire from his family to become a *samnyâsin sannyasi*, an adept of 'total abnegation', devoting himself, in perfect continence, to his spiritual calling.

It need hardly be said that such an ideal is not biblical. For the Bible, 'man leaves father and mother to cleave to his wife' (Gen 2:24; cf Mt 19:5; Mk 10:7), but no one leaves his wife.[1] On the contrary, he who dismisses his wife is responsible for her adulteries and is himself a fornicator (Mt 5:32; 19:9; Lk 16:18; Mk 10:11). The matrimonial union is a divine bond and nobody may loose it (Mt 19:6; Mk 10:9). Our knowledge of the life of the early Church is only fragmentary but as far as it goes it does not warrant the assertion that early Christians were advised to leave their wives for religious reasons 'except for a time, to devote themselves to prayer' (I Cor 7:5). It might be argued that the apostles are said to have abandoned 'everything' to follow Jesus (Lk 5:11, 28; Mt 19:27; Mk 10:28), but apparently 'everything' did not include their wives, since afterwards they were accompanied by them in their apostolic journeys (I Cor

---

[1] It is noticeable that when developing the theme of the superiority of God's love over family bonds, rabbinical literature does not mention the wife among the family loyalties that must be set aside when conflicting with the service of God. The only instance, in Josephus (*Ant. Jud.* xi, 5, 4), refers to the special case of the mixed marriages at the time of Nehemias. Cf *Str.-Bil.* I, p. 587.

9:5).[1] The view of the early Church in that respect is clearly stated by St Paul: 'For those who are married, my instructions are—and they are not mine, they are the Lord's— . . . the husband must not put away his wife' (I Cor 7:10f, 17, 27).[2] St Paul does not know of any exceptions. It would be quite surprising if Luke intended to defend or to introduce a custom so alien to biblical and apostolic tradition.

Therefore it must be concluded that Luke did not propose to the disciple of Christ conjugal separation as an ideal. The verb 'to give up' must be taken in an analogical way. Relatives and belongings must be properly left, or put away: man necessarily has them, and total detachment implies their abandon. But the case is different with a wife. Marriage it not necessary: it is a freely accepted relationship and the way to renounce it consists in not contracting it. To renounce a wife means simply to abstain from marriage. The disciple is not invited to give up *his* wife but *a* wife, to renounce the very prospect of having a wife. It is the ideal of celibacy that Luke evokes by his addition in 18:29.

By analogy, the same interpretation must be extended to 14:26. There, also, the meaning of the words cannot be discovered by reference to the immediate context, since they do not really belong to it, but rather to Luke's views on

[1] I Cor 9:5 alludes to the custom of several apostles of moving about with 'a woman, a sister' (ἀδελφὴν γυναῖκα). There is a certain reluctance among Catholic commentators (Rees, Callan, Ricciotti, Spicq, Prat, Osty, etc.) to see a wife in that 'woman' (cf the footnote in Knox' version; Allo hesitates). A 'sister' is a Christian woman (I Cor 7:15; Rom 16:1; Phm 2). If γυναῖκα does not mean wife, why that tautology of a 'lady Christian woman'? In a pagan world where scandals were many and suspicion easy, the apostles would have had enough common sense not to travel with a 'sister' who was not their wife.
[2] The verb used by Paul for 'putting away' is ἀφιέναι, exactly as in Lk 18:29.

perfect discipleship. Here too the idea is that the disciple should 'hate', should scorn, not his wife but married life. Plummer suggests that Luke's insertion of wife is 'a comment, whether designed or not, on v. 20'.[1] In that verse of the parable of the banquet, one of the guests excuses himself on the ground that he has just taken a wife and finds himself unable to come. V. 26 draws the lesson: the disciple should not place himself in that situation: he must not take a wife. Here again, 'to hate wife and children' means to reject the idea of having them, to reject the very prospect of being entangled by them in one's effort to follow Christ till the end. The disciple scorns his family by not clinging to it but, of course, he cannot avoid belonging to a family. He scorns wife and children by remaining a celibate.

It might be objected to this interpretation that it supposes encratist tendencies in Luke. Celibacy seems to be considered as a necessary condition of discipleship, with the additional difficulty that, by disciples of Christ, Luke understood all Christians (cf Ac 6:1; 9:19; 11:26). Are we to suppose that Luke made of celibacy an indispensable requirement of Christian life? Some allowance must be made for Luke's oratorical tendencies. A few verses later (14:33), Luke says similarly that, if one does not renounce all one's possessions, one cannot be a disciple. Does he mean that private property is incompatible with Christian life? Luke knew well enough that among Jesus' followers there were Marthas who continued to live their ordinary life in the world with its material problems (Lk 10:38-42; 8:3). True, his descriptions of the Christian communities in the Acts would leave the impression of a kind of total communism in the early days of the Church (2:44f; 4:32, 34f). Yet the story of Ananias makes it clear

[1] *Op. cit.*, p. 364.

59

that such total dispossession of one's personal belongings was not deemed a necessary condition to entry into the Church (Ac 5:4). 'There is a strong element of generalization in those descriptions . . . Luke has a tendency to give an absolute ring to the requirements of self-denial contained in the message of the Gospel. This tendency led him to retouch slightly but significantly the sources on which he worked to compose his Gospel.'[1] But when retouching his sources to propose celibacy so radically to Christ's disciples, Luke did not ignore the sanctity of marriage. He meant only to draw an ideal picture of the perfect disciple, knowing well that there are degrees in generosity and diversity in charismatic gifts, and that there are particular circumstances that cannot always be overlooked. Of Luke's invitation to celibacy may be said what Plummer wrote of Jesus' call to self-denial: 'as often, (he) states a principle in a startling way and leaves his hearers to find out the qualifications'.[2]

Luke, the disciple of Paul, had understood the exhortation of his master: 'I would that all men were like me (unmarried) . . . and I say to the unmarried, it would be better for them to remain so, as I am myself' (I Cor 7:7f). Luke must himself have remained a celibate, as an old tradition has it.[3] By inserting in the Gospel an invitation to celibacy, he echoed the call of his master to attain perfection by perfect continence (I Cor 7:1).

In a way, Luke was even more accurate than Paul when he attributed the call to Jesus himself. When asked by the Corinthians how to deal with the problem of the virgins and

[1] J. Dupont, op. cit., pp. 195f.
[2] Op. cit., p. 364.
[3] A tradition which, according to Lagrange (op. cit., pp. xiv-xvii), goes back at least to the second century.

widows, St Paul had not been able to remember any decision of Christ on that topic (I Cor 7:25). Luke the evangelist knew the sayings of the Lord better. It was true that Jesus had given no precept on that question, but he had thrown out a suggestion. Luke knew that Jesus had proposed the ideal of virginity to those 'who could understand'. For instance there had been the saying on the eunuchs (Mt 19:12). Luke had omitted this from his Gospel on account of its bluntness, for fear of offending his Gentile readers, unused to the uncouth rhetoric of Israel.[1] But he could not omit the lesson. It was too important. It corresponded too well with his spirituality and his concept of perfect discipleship. The discreet allusions to celibacy which he added to the sayings on self-denial were for him a way of making up for the text he had to omit for stylistic reasons.[2]

2. *A daily cross*

Luke's minute additions to the two sayings on self-denial are his rendering of the logion on the spiritual eunuchs. But there is more in this than a simple transposition: it is not only a matter of toning down too crude a style. The change was more than stylistic: by the fact that Luke gave a different context to Jesus' invitation to celibacy, to some extent he gave it a new meaning; or at least, by giving it another background, he threw a new light on its value.

In the logion on the eunuchs, celibacy had been given mostly an eschatological meaning: 'he that could understand' had been invited to anticipate on earth the conditions that would prevail in the imminent Kingdom.[3] Luke knew

[1] Cf p. 39.
[2] Cf E. Osty, *L'Evangile selon St Luc (BJ)*, Paris 1948, p. 23.
[3] Cf ch 2.

that teaching. In 18:29 he echoed it almost literally by advising celibacy 'for the sake of God's Kingdom'. These words are proper to Lk and, since they are the very words of Mt 19:12, it is likely that Luke introduced them to hint at the logion on the eunuchs. Yet there is a change of standpoint. The celibate 'for the sake of the Kingdom' is so, in Lk, not so much to anticipate the life to come, as to proclaim in a more compelling way the significance of the present period in the history of salvation. Aware that this is the time when the Kingdom of the poor has been installed (18:24), to enter which one has to dispossess oneself of any worldly hope or tie, the disciple, according to Lk 18:29, embraces virginity as an example of the poverty required to enter the Kingdom of the *anawim*. In the same manner the Magnificat (Lk 1:48), to describe Mary's condition as a virgin, had used the word ταπείνωσις.[1]

Lk 14:26 reveals the foundation of the doctrine by resolving the poverty of the Kingdom into the mystery of the cross. The supreme poverty is that of the cross, and virginity is presented as a way of sharing in the utter dispossession of self which Christ realized on Calvary. The reason given for celibacy is that the disciple must carry the cross with Jesus: celibacy becomes a part of the process of mortification by which we share in the mystery and the efficacy of the cross.

When connecting renunciation of earthly ties with the necessity of carrying the cross, Luke followed his source. But, as usual, while keeping as close as possible to his source, he interpreted it with great originality of thought. The words were mostly those of the source, much the same as those found in the parallel text of Mt and also in the context of the

[1]Cf p.124.

'Markan tradition' where the same saying recurs (Mk 8:34; Mt 16:24; Lk 9:23). But Luke infused into them his own deep understanding of the Christian mystery.

In the source, and still in Mt and Mk, the carrying of the cross was taken in a literal sense; it was understood in the sense which the Jews must have given it when they had heard Jesus utter that sentence. At that stage the cross had no mystic or symbolic connotation.[1] It was the material cross, the *patibulum* which those who had been condemned to death by the Roman régime could frequently be seen carrying to the place of their execution. The genuine authenticity of the logion has been suspected on the ground that it is too 'Christian', or even too 'Pauline', really to belong to Jesus' ministry; it is alleged that it supposes a theology of the cross which could not be expected of the 'historical Jesus' or at least which Jesus could not have expected of his audience.[2] But this objection is based on a misunderstanding of the saying in its original sense. There is no theology in it; there is nothing more than an allusion to the pitiful sight which was fairly common in any province of the Roman Empire in those days. As V. Taylor remarks: 'Death by crucifixion under the Romans was a sufficiently familiar sight in Palestine to be the basis of the saying.'[3]

---

[1]The cross does not seem to have been given the symbolic meaning of hardship in Palestine at the time of our Lord; old rabbinical literature never uses the phrase 'to carry the cross' in the metaphorical sense of undergoing great trials. Cf *Str.-Bil.* I, p. 587. In *Genesis rabba* 56, 36c, there is a reference to Isaac carrying the wood of the sacrifice 'as somebody who carries the cross on his shoulders'. But (against Bultmann, *op. cit.*, p. 173n) there is no need to understand the allusion in a metaphorical sense.

[2]Cf A. Loisy, *Les Evangiles Synoptiques*, I, Ceffonds 1907, p. 895.

[3]*The Gospel according to St Mark*, London 1955, p. 381. Even Bultmann would accept the historicity of the saying: *op. cit.*, p. 173.

The pronouncement might even have derived from a grim Zealotist slogan.[1] In the context of the Galilean ministry, it need not be supposed that Jesus, when speaking of carrying the cross, meant a mystical union with his death: 'At that stage, Jesus had not yet spoken about his passion: he could not therefore allude to his own execution.'[2] What he meant and what the Jews understood was that the disciples had to be ready to face the greatest risks, to face death and even the appalling death on the cross. This literal sense of the cross is still preserved in the context of Mt and Mk. In Mk 8:34 and Mt 16:24, Christ exhorts his followers not to mind their own life. In Mt 10:38, as we have already said, the discourse refers to the eschatological struggle: it may divide families, it may even cost the disciples their lives: they must be ready to face the prospect of having to join the frightful procession of the *furciferi* dragged across the streets to their death. In that context, the saying on severing family ties and the saying on carrying the cross do not explain each other. They are only parallel examples of the severity of the crisis through which the disciples must be ready to pass.

In Luke, on the contrary, the eschatological context has disappeared. The question now concerns the obligations of discipleship. It implies total renouncement, utmost self-denial. It is a life of sacrifice that can be compared to a way of the cross. The saying on detachment and the saying on the cross explain each other. The cross is not the *patibulum* that the disciple may have to shoulder; it is the mystical cross of the hardships of his life, and the sacrifices by which he unites himself with the death of his Master.

---

[1]This is the suggestion of A. Schlatter, *Der Evangelist Matthaüs*, Stuttgart 1933, pp. 35of.
[2]M. J. Lagrange, *St Matthieu*, p. 213.

That Luke understood the cross of the disciple in this mystical sense clearly appears from his rendering of the logion in the Markan context. As given by Matthew and Mark, the text was an invitation to martyrdom. 'Luke added the words καθ' ἡμέραν to the logion: "let him take the cross *daily*" (9:23). This small addition transforms the whole atmosphere. It is every day, in their daily life, that Christians will find the opportunity to imitate their Master. It is by carrying those daily crosses that they will renounce their own life, and will save it by losing it; probably we may even translate: they will save their soul.'[1]

The cross is no more the cross of physical persecutions; it consists in the daily mortifications by which one applies to oneself the mystery of the death of Christ. In Lk 14:27 it may be that this conception explains the verb used by Luke for 'carrying' the cross. Instead of the commonplace λαμβάνειν (*to take:* Mt 10:38) or αἴρειν (*to take up:* Mk 8:34), Luke chose the rarer verb βαστάζειν (*to bear a burden*). It has been remarked that this verb is preferred in biblical Greek when the carrying is figurative (IV Kg 18:14; Job 21:3 according to the *codex Alexandrinus*).[2] It is also the verb used by John to describe the way of the cross (19:17). There is the possibility that John might have had in view precisely the logion on carrying the cross: Jesus was doing 'for himself' what he had advised the disciples to do.[3] Conversely it might be said that by using the rare verb βαστάζειν, Luke referred to the carrying of the cross by Jesus. The use of that verb would be one more instance of the contacts with

---

[1] L. Cerfaux, 'Fructifiez en supportant l'epreuve', in *RB* 64 (1957), p. 489.
[2] A. Plummer, *op. cit.*, p. 364.
[3] M.-J. Lagrange, *Evangile selon St Jean*, Paris 1948, pp. 490f.

the Johannine tradition which have been noticed as one of the peculiarities of Luke's Gospel.[1] If such a contact does exist, the disciples and Jesus, in Lk and in Jn, are shown doing the same thing: Jesus, carrying the cross, brings to fulfilment the abnegation he asked from his disciples and the disciples actualize in their daily life the mystery of salvation contained in the cross.

This reference to John's thought may be questioned. But, on the contrary, the Pauline background of Luke's rendering of the logion can hardly be doubted. Between the saying on carrying the cross in its original sense and its interpretation by Luke, there is Paul's conception of Christian life: 'I have been crucified with Christ' (Gal 2:19). Christian life consists in a mystical union with Christ. Through faith and sacraments a mystical bond is established between us and the dead and risen Lord (Rom 6:3-6). Hence our destinies and our very body and spirit are patterned upon the likeness of Christ's death and resurrection: we are dead to the flesh and its allies (Rom 6:7-11; 7:4). We live in the Spirit and of the Spirit, no longer do we depend on the flesh, though we still live in the flesh; for we are of the Spirit (Rom 8:5-13). The old man in us has been crucified with Christ: 'We carry about everywhere in our body the putting to death (νέκρωσις) of Jesus. Though alive, we are continuously given over to death for Jesus' sake . . . Death is active in us' (II Cor 4:10-12). It is not only the Eucharist which announces the death of the Lord, 'recalls' it and makes it present. In another way, the daily life of Christians, with its tribulations, anxieties, persecutions and shattering blows does so also (II Cor 4:9).

[1] Cf F. M. Braun, *La Mère des Fidèles*, Tournai-Paris 1954, pp. 26-30; D. Mollat, *L'Evangile et les Epîtres de St Jean (BJ)*, Paris 1953, p. 39.

It is easy to recognize here the principles underlying Luke's spirituality of the daily cross. Taught by Paul, Luke perceived in the saying on carrying the cross the depth it was to have when understood in the light of Jesus' death and resurrection. The saying, in its full sense, was no mere rhetorical invitation to follow the Master till the end. It was a programme of Christian life that gave a mystical value to the manifold hardships a disciple has to endure. Those trials Luke knew by experience: he knew the heart-rending decisions which a follower of Christ has to make, against his own interests and affections. And he knew that celibacy was one of the most 'crucifying' forms of self-denial, one of the most absolute ways of taking on the νέκρωσις of Jesus. By renouncing wife and children, the disciple was enabled to strip the 'body of flesh' most completely, not in any encratistic sense, as if the body and its use were unclean by nature (cf Rom 14:14, 20), but in the sense in which St Paul had spoken of a total circumcision of the whole flesh (Col 2:11): stripping of self, death with Christ and renunciation of any kind of merely human comfort and support. By embracing celibacy, one sets aside earthly ties and even the desire to have descendants and to see one's destiny prolonged and rejuvenated in one's children. This desire is not sinful: it is deeply rooted in human nature and it corresponds to the divine ordinance (Gen 1:28). Yet still it is reliance on the flesh and it still belongs to the fleeting world; it is still this side of the cosmic transformation, of the 'newness of life' initially realized through the death and resurrection of Christ. The disciple who has understood the *verbum crucis* has no other hope than that which shines beyond the Cross. Because he knows only Christ and him crucified, he takes the cross and the cross of virginity. Virginity becomes for him the radical way to carry to the utmost the νέκρωσις which is required by his fellowship with a crucified Master.

If our analysis is correct, Luke's view on Christian celibacy embodies a theological development. In the sources he used, Jesus' invitation to forgo marriage and procreation for the sake of the Kingdom was based on eschatological considerations: the Kingdom was at hand and so the times had come for those to whom it had been given to cut themselves clear of worldly entanglements and thus to show forth in their lives the conditions prevailing in the new aeon. In Lk, eschatological considerations are not excluded, but they are resolved into the present reality. Celibacy is linked with the meaning of Christian life, which is a 'life in Christ', consisting in imitation of and identification with the Master. And this is realized by shaping our destiny on the pattern of the cross, since it is on the cross that Christ completed his mission by assuming most fully his solidarity with the humanity of flesh, bringing it to the point where it would be ready to turn, by the power of the Spirit, into a humanity of glory. Celibacy announces the cross: it not only indicates that the times have come for the final decision by which one enters the New Kingdom: it is the outward sign of a mystery which is now at work in us, the mystery of life and death by which the Passion and the resurrection of Christ are continued in his body, which is the Church.

Thus, in the outlook of the early Church on the cross and virginity, there was a shift from eschatological hopes to a mystical view of our life 'in Christ'. It is this shift which Mgr Cerfaux has traced in the whole development of St Paul's thought on the mystery of Christ.[1] As Mgr Cerfaux

[1] L. Cerfaux, *Christ in the Theology of St Paul*, Edinburgh 1958; for a general synopsis of the main thesis of the book, see pp. 529-534.

has done in the case of the doctrine of St Paul, it must be emphasized that from the earliest conceptions of Christian celibacy to that of Luke, the development was homogeneous. Following Paul, Luke did not give up the eschatological conceptions of Christian life. But he deepened it, and stressed that the final decision in favour of the New Kingdom and of the new life in the Spirit was to be a matter of daily occurrence. Daily one has to side against this world and renew one's allegiance to the Kingdom. As regards celibacy also, it is daily that through it one dies to the world of flesh. Luke knew by personal experience that it is not simply a state of life one enters once for all by a single decision; it implies a continuous renewal of the choice once made and it is a continuous mortification.

It was to be the role of Paul and Luke to explain to the early Church the full meaning of the message of Jesus concerning the cross. Jesus had taught that the eschatological fight and victory had to be primarily interior, consisting essentially in a change of heart. Paul understood that the death on the cross was the fulfilment of that programme: he saw in the cross the sign of that change of condition, of the passage from the world of flesh to the world of the Spirit. Thus the cross had a universal significance. It had not only to be carried through the streets of Jerusalem; it had to encompass the world and mark every human destiny. Luke applied that doctrine to Christian celibacy. For him dedicated celibacy shows the impact of the cross on the individual lives of the faithful. It is the sign of the cross deeply marked in the flesh and in the body and soul of the faithful. It is a cross in the most radical sense. Or rather it is *the* cross. The mystical carrying of the cross which Paul and Luke attributed to the disciple should not be taken as merely allegorical.

For all the mystical value he gave to the cross, Luke, like Paul, did not idealize or allegorize it; he did not make of it a tame comparison to express any kind of annoyance or discomfort. For Luke, the cross was still the cross, an object of infamy, anguish and forlorn abandon. It was the same when applied to continence. It is actually on the frightening gallows of Calvary that virgins have to live. Those who follow Jesus till the end must know that their celibacy is a cross, is even *the* cross, like martyrdom. Luke would have accepted the stern description Methodius of Olympus gave of the life of the Christian virgins:

'They underwent a martyrdom: for it is not just a short time that they had to endure physical torments; a whole lifetime they bore the strain. They did not hesitate to face the truly Olympian fight of chastity, resisting by force the savage assault of pleasures, fears and sorrows and the other forms of man's wickedness.'[1]

Celibacy is a fight, an ἀγών, like Christ's passion. It may entail all the pangs and anguish Christ experienced on the cross. But the Christian virgins are comforted by the knowledge that the pains of their state of life are nothing but the pains of the death of their Master, the birth-pains of the new world, of the progressive stripping of the flesh from the old man, as the new Adam rises slowly to the new life in the Spirit.

---

[1]*Convivium Decem Virginum* vii, 3 (*PG* 18, 128). On the theme of celibacy as a deadly combat, see J. Steinmann, *Saint John and the Desert Tradition*, London 1955, pp. 159-167.

CHAPTER FOUR

Virginity as an Apotheosis

WHEN ACHIMELEK the priest of Nob offered the shewbread of his sanctuary to David and his hungry companions, he made one condition: the men, he told David, should 'have kept themselves from women'. 'Indeed,' replied David to the priest, 'women have been kept away from us, as always when I take the field: the bodies of my men are holy. This may be a profane journey; yet today they are holy in their bodies.'[1] Upon which assurance, Achimelek distributed the 'holy bread' (I Sam 21:4-6).

This episode gives two cases in which temporary continence was required in the Old Testament: before eating sacred food,[2] and when engaged in a military expedition.[3]

[1]The Hebrew text of the second part of David's reply is not clear. We follow here the translation proposed by R. de Vaux, *Les Livres de Samuel* (*BJ*), Paris, 1953 p. 102. Though it makes clumsy English, we translate the Hebrew *qâdôsh* by 'holy'. 'Clean' or 'pure' would be more idiomatic (cf Knox version) but would miss the point. The Hebrew word for 'body' is *keli*: thing, utensil, body. Here it may be a euphemism, as 'parts' in English.

[2]At least it must have been so at the time of David. The later legislation of Lev 22:2-7 does not include normal marital relations among the impediments which bar the Israelite from a sacred meal.

[3]This law also explains the behaviour of Urias, refusing to enter his house and see his wife when he was summoned by David to Jerusalem (II Sam 11:8-13). At Qumran, continence is expected of those who will take part in the apocalyptic 'War of the Children of Light against the Children

The text shows also that the purpose of this practice was to confer physical 'holiness' on those who observed it.

Similarly, in his defence of virginity in I Cor 7, St Paul says that the aim of the virgin is 'to be holy in body and in spirit' (v. 34). For Paul also, continence is connected with 'holiness': the parallelism with the Old Testament concept is obvious.

What is that 'sanctity' which St Paul and the Old Law saw in continence? The term 'holiness' has very wide and varying implications in the Bible. How are we to understand the 'holiness' that gives a distinct value to continence and virginity?

1. *Continence and cult in the Old Testament*

Another case of temporary continence in the Old Testament is to be found in Ex 19:14f where the Israelites, at the foot of Mt Sinai, are requested to 'sanctify themselves' by three days of continence before the ratification of the Covenant and the promulgation of the Law.

The explanation that comes spontaneously to the mind is that it was a matter of ritual cleanness. Marital relations would entail a defilement and had therefore to be omitted before celebrating the rites of the Covenant or receiving sacred food. The same explanation would account also for continence in time of war. The Israelites considered military campaigns as a kind of liturgy. Wars were sacred; they were, as the old Hebrew poem has it, 'the wars of Yahweh' (Num

of Darkness' (vii, 3) (cf above p. 21). If celibacy was kept at least in some sections of the Essene sect, one reason might have been the consciousness that, by entering the Community, they had joined the camp of God; they were on a war footing and, for them, the eschatological war had already started.

21:14; cf I Sam 18:17; 25:28). Yahweh encamped with his troops (Jg 4:14; II Sam 5:24). Hence the whole camp was 'holy' (Dt 23:10-15), transformed into a sanctuary by the presence of the Ark (cf Num 10:35f; I Sam 4) and warriors were the 'sanctified of Yahweh' (Is 13:3; cf Jer 22:7; 51:27f).[1] This ritual background of war is obviously the reason for the temporary continence observed by David and his companions: it had the same significance as that of the Israelites standing at the foot of Sinai. The cult put the people in the divine presence or in contact with objects dedicated to God and, for that, ritual cleanness had to be observed.

Because it stresses the cultic significance of continence, this explanation contains an important element of truth. But is it correct to express the matter in terms of 'cleanness'? It should be noticed that in the Bible the use of marriage does not seem to be considered as a cause of defilement.[2] Moreover, the texts under consideration do not describe continence as clean (in Hebrew, *ṭâhôr*) but as holy (*qâdôsh*); the opposite condition is profane (*ḥol*), not unclean (*ṭâmê'*): there is no 'profane' bread, says Achimelek, but only the 'holy' shewbread; so the men must be 'holy' and David has to certify that, though the circumstances of the journey may be 'profane', his men are indeed 'holy'.

There is a great difference between cleanness and—even physical—holiness.[3] Cleanness was essentially a negative

---

[1] Cf R. de Vaux, *Les Institutions de l'Ancien Testament* II, Paris 1960, p. 74; J. Pedersen, *op. cit.*, III-IV, London 1940, pp. 12-15.

[2] Defilement was caused not by the use of marriage but by certain sexual phenomena which evoked a loss of physical integrity, as did leprosy or gonorrhoea, with which they were listed (Lev 22:4-8).

[3] In spite of the fact that, by a process of association, on account of the practical similarities between the two notions, the words are sometimes interchanged: Jos 7:13; II Sam 11:4; Job 1:5; Dt 22:9; Ez 23:38f.

notion: it consisted in the absence or in the removal of any cause of defilement.[1] Holiness, on the contrary, had a positive value. Coming from a root which probably contained the idea of separation, the word *qâdôsh*, particularly when, as in I Sam 21:4ff, it was used in opposition to *ḥol*, meant 'that which differed' from the familiar course of things; that which, taken above the level of profane existence, shared in the awesome aloofness of the divine majesty. Holiness was a kind of metaphysical radiance that made the reality which was impregnated with it at the same time fascinating and dangerous.[2] For the Hebrews, it was strictly speaking a divine attribute and even 'so to say the very essence of the divinity'.[3] Sanctification was therefore a kind of assumption into the divine sphere.

It was the purpose of the cult to bring about that 'sanctification'. The cult was the activity by which man put himself in the divine presence, expecting God to answer, to come and meet him, as he had met Israel on the occasion of the great events which the cult commemorated. This cultic contact with

[1] According to the Semitic mentality, it is the unclean which has a positive meaning: uncleanness is a quality which affects the object, just as holiness does. In the two antitheses holy-profane and clean-unclean, it is the terms holy and unclean which are positive, profane and clean being merely the negation of the quality implied in the opposite term: 'Dans la mentalité ancienne, l'impur et le sacré sont des notions connexes. Ils contiennent l'un et l'autre une force mystérieuse et effrayante, qui agit par contact et qui met en état d'interdit . . . Ces conceptions primitives se retrouvent dans l'Ancien Testament: on ne peut pas toucher l'Arche d'alliance et on ne peut pas toucher un cadavre; la mère doit se purifier après l'accouchement, qui l'a rendue impure, et le prêtre doit changer ses vêtements après le sacrifice, qui l'a rendu sacré' (R. de Vaux, *op. cit.*, p. 353). On the distinction between the notion of holiness and that of purity, cf O. Procksch in *TWNT* I, p. 88, and P. van Imschoot, *Théologie de l'Ancien Testament*, II, Paris-Tournai 1956, pp. 204f.

[2] Cf R. Otto, *The Idea of the Holy*, Oxford 1923.

[3] P. van Imschoot, *op. cit.*, I, 1954, p. 42.

God impregnated with divine 'holiness' the things and the people who took part in the liturgy. Set apart from profane existence, they were impregnated with divine radiation and raised up into the sphere of the divine glory. Thus they acquired, at least for a time, a special quality which made them unfit for profane life. Such was especially the case of the ministers of the cult. 'Sanctified' by the divine contact, they were set apart; they had to keep aloof from the routine of daily life and this aloofness was the mark left upon them by their contact with the holiness of God. Like Moses on Mt Sinai, away from the routines of daily life, they communed with the divine glory on the religious summits to which the 'Most High' had taken them.

Continence was part of that process of 'sanctification'. As the Levite was, at least theoretically, exempted from tilling the land so as to be entirely at the service of God (Jos 13:14, 33; 14:3f; 18:7), so the Israelite engaging in the performance of the cult had to leave the profane world behind and even the profane duty of procreation, so as to stand in attendance before Yahweh and commune in the sacred atmosphere surrounding the deity.

The temporary continence of the Old Testament was therefore a case, not exactly of ritual cleanliness, but of cultic consecration. Its aim was not to remove a stain but to manifest the intensity of man's dedication to God's affairs and the assumption of his life into a higher sphere. It signified that man had left his earthly abode to be transferred into the divine presence. Thus in Jl 2:16, the prophet invites the 'bridegroom to go forth from his bed and the bride out of her bride-chamber' in order to attend a ceremony of lamentation on the occasion of a national calamity. The context shows clearly the meaning of that invitation to continence: it is not that there would be anything unseemly about conjugal relations in such sad circumstances; nor is it supposed that continence would be a praiseworthy act of mortification that might help to placate God. The intention is rather, as the Hebrew text has it, to 'sanctify' an assembly; the people must go and meet God in the temple. Hence, for the time being, they have to leave their profane occupations and enter the divine presence. Fasting also is part of that process by which existence is loosed from its profane moorings and given a sacral value (cf 2:15 and 1:14: 'sanctify a fast'). Continence has the same meaning.

Other cases of cultic continence betray the same purpose. According to the Mishna, 'the High Priest was taken away from home and placed in the council room' seven days before the celebration of the Day of Atonement.[1] The Mishnaic treatise explains the rule in terms of ritual cleanliness 'for fear that "an accident" might happen, rendering him unfit for his functions'. But the original intention must have been deeper: the priest had to be 'away from home', that is, free from profane commitments, and be entirely concerned with his sacred business. The seven days of isolation before the feast were meant to prepare him for that consecration: it was a 'holy' time, a time devoted to God. So also was the time of the priestly ordination, on the occasion of which, for seven days, Aaron and his sons—and presumably later on the clergy of Jerusalem—had to stay 'day and night at the entrance of the sanctuary' (Lev 8:33). Evidently this entailed continence, but it is noteworthy that continence is not explicitly mentioned in that text. It has no special interest in itself. The point is that the new priest must, so to say, offer to God the first-fruits of his priestly

[1] *Yoma* 1, 1; quoted in *Text. Rab.*, no. 880, p. 218.

existence by staying in the sanctuary, entirely given to his cultic meeting with God.[1] Continence is only an implicit aspect of that dedication.

It is for the same cultic reason that, according to a school of Rabbis,[2] marital relations were forbidden on the sabbath day: sabbath was sacred time. The work of procreation was as profane as any other work; it was included among those activities, good indeed and blessed by God, yet profane, by which man was to 'fill the earth and subdue it' (Gen 1:28).[3] On the seventh day, such activities had to be interrupted so as to draw near to God through the cult, and share in the divine rest.

According to the commentary of Rabbi Nathan on the *Pirquê Aboth*, the sabbath evoked the Day of the Messias, 'the day that will be entirely sabbath, when there is no eating nor drinking, buying nor selling; but the just will remain sitting with their crowns on their head and will enjoy the

---

[1]Quoting Lev 8:33 as an anticipation of Christian priestly celibacy, the encyclical *Ad Catholici Sacerdotii* observes that the Roman religion also knew the principle *ad deos adeunto caste* (*AAS* 28, 1936, p. 25). The encyclical quotes also the interesting commentary of Cicero on that principle (*De Legibus* II, 8).

[2]Cf *Text. Rab.*, no. 1256, p. 232 (*Ketuboth, Talmud Babli*, 65b).

[3]It should be noticed that, from the standpoint of the Bible, 'profane' does not mean deprived of any religious significance. In the life of Israel, the Covenant is brought to bear upon everything and so everything has a religious value. The concept of 'profane', being negative, is relative. The land is profane because it is deprived of the special holiness of the Temple; yet, by comparison with the pagan lands, it is sacred (Dt 11: 10-17). The week is profane because it has not the special sanctity of the sabbath; yet work has a sacred value by carrying on the Creation (Ex 20:8-11). Continence shares in the supreme sanctity of the cultic realities which belong directly to God. By comparison, matrimony and procreation are profane. Yet they also have a sacred value since it is actually through them that God's plan is carried out in the offspring of Abraham. On the sacrality of matrimony, see P. Grelot, *Le Couple humain dans l'Ecriture*, Paris 1961.

splendour of the *Shekinah*'.[1] If Rabbi Nathan had added 'begetting' to the list of the works which are not done during the eternal rest and its ritual anticipation on the sabbath day,[2] he would have given the exact meaning of cultic continence: profane life is suspended while the just take their rest, entranced and fascinated by the divine radiance shining through the cult. In that rapture, they might say with the psalmist:

> Whom else have I in heaven but You?
> and when I am with You, the earth delights me not.
> My flesh and my heart are spent,
> God is my portion forever . . .
> For me, my joy is to be with God. (Ps 73:25-28)

Commentators consider this text to be one of the highest expressions of love for God in the Old Testament.[3] The pious Israelite would recognize in it also the best explanation of his 'sanctification' through the cult, and of the continence this sanctification entailed at those times: there is no thought even for the earthly joys and duties of marriage when, in the cult, flesh and heart are consumed by the terrifying joy of facing the dazzling presence of the divine *Shekinah*.

2. *Virginity and the cult of the New Testament*

The days of the Messias have come. With the advent of

---

[1]*Aboth de Rabbi Nathan* I; cf *Str.-Bil.* I, p. 890.

[2]This description of the just with a crown on their head, sitting in the light of the *Shekinah*, was a cliché of rabbinical literature. See texts in *Str.-Bil.*, ibid. Used to describe the life of the world to come, it included 'begetting and procreating' among the things that would not be done any more in that age. Applying the theme to the sabbath, R. Nathan omitted these words, possibly because he did not belong to the school that forbade marital relations on the sabbath day.

[3]Cf E. Podechard, *Le Psautier, Traduction Littérale et Explication Historique*, I, Lyon 1949, p. 319.

Christ the divine presence is no longer hidden behind the veils of cultic symbols: it abides with us and the glory of the *Shekinah* shines in the flesh of the Incarnate Word (Jn 1:14). The believer lives continually in the radiance of that presence: his whole life may realize what the old cult had only prepared and typified.

As regards continence, the consequences of the new dispensation were already suggested in a midrashic text which said:

> If on the day when God manifested himself on Mt Sinai to give the Law, he forbade marital intercourse for three days, will not the same be forbidden also in the age to come when the *Shekinah* will abide with them?[1]

The midrash was wrong in putting the matter in terms of prohibition: marriage is not evil that it should be forbidden. It must rather fade away by itself when the conditions have changed. Virginity does not belong to the Law that compels but to the Spirit that prompts 'sweetly and firmly'. Yet in his clumsy way the midrashic author shows an interesting insight into the meaning of virginity. When the days of the Messias have come and the *Shekinah* has been manifested in him, cultic continence can be fulfilled. Man can fully dedicate his life to the joy of living in the divine presence and, in that joy, forego marriage and family. Virginity in the New Testament extends to the whole of human life the 'holiness' which the Old Testament saw already in temporary continence. It is in that sense that St Paul in I Cor 7:34 described virginity as a condition of physical and spiritual 'holiness'.

The aim of the Christian celibate is to 'be holy both in

[1] *Midrash Ps* 146 §4 in *Str.-Bil.* I, p. 889. Cf Mk 12:25.

body and in spirit'. It would be a complete misunderstanding of Paul's thought to give holiness in that text its modern meaning of moral perfection. This meaning should not be assumed too easily. Undoubtedly virginity, implying perfect self-control, brings along with it all the other virtues. As St Jerome says, repeating a formula which ultimately goes back to Socrates,[1] 'continence is the strong foundation and the lofty pinnacle of all virtues: it supports and protects them all'.[2] But true as this may be, this moral view of virginity was not in Paul's mind when he exhorted the Corinthians to celibacy. In the writings of the Apostle as in the rest of the Bible, 'holiness' is not primarily a moral quality. Ἅγιος in the Greek of the New Testament, as qâdôsh in the Hebrew of the Old, does not mean virtuous, good or pious but, as we saw, sacred. Its connotations are basically not ethical but religious. Moreover, in the context of I Cor 7:34, the merely ethical meaning of the word is excluded by the sentence itself, which speaks of physical and spiritual sanctity: moral sanctity cannot be physical.

The reference to 'bodily sanctity' shows the cultic background of St Paul's thought. Yet, still less than in the continence of the old cult should that physical holiness be reduced to mere cleanness. In the context of I Cor 7, virginity is opposed to marriage, but marriage for Paul is not unclean. When he wrote I Cor, he may not yet have had in mind the spirituality of matrimony he was to develop in Eph 5:25-33. But he did not consider wedlock as unholy. Just before writing on virginity, when drawing the consequences of the

---

[1] As reported by Xenophon, *Mem.* 1, 5, 4. The formula was borrowed by Philo (*De Specialibus Legibus* iv, 101) and had some success among the Fathers of the Church. Cf P. T. Camelot, art. 'Enkrateia' in *Dictionnaire de Spiritualité*, fasc. xxv, Paris 1958, col 357-370.
[2] *Adv. Jov.* I, 38: *PL* 23, 264b.

principle that our bodies are the members of Christ, he does not conclude that it would be repugnant to imagine the limbs of Christ engaged in married life. Fornication only would be abhorrent in the Body of Christ (I Cor 6:15-20). Matrimony does not defile. Only sin does.

Matrimony is not sinful. But it is profane.[1] It belongs to the 'things of this world', to the fleeting realities of our present condition (I Cor 7:32ff). The opposition between virginity and matrimony is not that of purity and impurity. As in the Old Testament, they are contrasted as sacred and profane life. Virginity is 'holy', that is sacred in the biblical sense of the term: it is *qâdôsh*, set apart and exalted. 'Dedicated'[2] or, rather, 'consecrated' would be the best rendering of the adjective ἅγιος in I Cor 7:34. By continence the virgin is made sacred, assumed into the sacred sphere of the divine glory.

Like the temporary continence of the Old Testament, Christian celibacy has a cultic connotation. It does not aim at a physical or moral cleanness but at a consecration. But now, in the New Testament, this consecration covers the whole life of the faithful, for now not only the Church (I Cor 3:17; Eph 2:21) but even the body of every Christian is a temple (I Cor 6:19; II Cor 6:16) enclosing the *Shekinah*, the divine presence. Christian life consists in a continuous liturgy in which God's presence is recognized and glorified (I Cor 6:20). Perpetual continence is the logical consequence of that permanent spiritual liturgy. To a higher degree than the rites of the Old Law, this new liturgy raises man above

[1]Especially as regards Christian marriage, this 'profane' character should be properly qualified. It is profane in a relative way, as far as it does not share in the special sanctity of virginity. But it is understood that it has also a sacred value, being even a sacrament of the New Covenant. Cf ch. 6, pp. 106ff.

[2]This is the term chosen by the New English Version.

6

ordinary life. It is given to some to spend their whole life in that 'better cult', 'the perfect cult of the living God' (Heb 9:14) which is part of the heavenly liturgy performed by the risen Christ: those are the virgins. With Christ, they 'have come not to the dark clouds' (of Sinai) but to the 'solemn feast' and to the radiance of the 'heavenly Jerusalem' (cf Heb 12:18-22). There the believer, with Christ, 'offers a cult pleasing to God with reverence and awe' (Heb 12:28). Virginity is the most active form of participation in that heavenly liturgy.

And because, in the New Covenant, priest and victim are identified, since now the offering is, in Christ, that of self, the holocaust which the virgins offer is 'the living holocaust of their bodies dedicated (ἅγια) to God' (Rom 12:1). In that respect also, virginity belongs to the new cult and is holy. Not only as a minister but also as a victim, the virgin is consecrated and raised to the sphere of the divine.[1]

To understand this sacrificial consecration of virginity, it must be remembered that, in the biblical sacrifices and especially in the holocaust, the victim was destroyed, but the destruction was not an end in itself. It was 'a way to place the offering in God by transferring it into the field of the

[1]Origen had already given the same explanation of I Cor 7:34. '... "That she may be holy both in body and in spirit": the fact that he (Paul) uses the word "holy" has this reference, that it is applied to people who are dedicated to God. Hence it is that the ram, for instance, which is dedicated to God is called holy and it is not allowed to shear it for profane use. A calf also, once dedicated to God, is called holy and it is not allowed to yoke it for profane work. We may understand from this what it is for man to dedicate himself to God. If you devote yourself to God, you must imitate the beast (offered in sacrifice) which must no longer serve human purposes, nor do anything whatsoever concerning men and the present life. But all that concerns the soul and observance of divine worship, that is what you must do and consider' (*Num. hom.* 24, 2: *PG* 12, 761b).

invisible'.[1] As appears from the Hebrew name of the holocaust (*'olah:* elevation), the disappearance of the victim was only the reverse side of its exaltation: 'The sacrifice was a transfer and a transformation. When on a solemn occasion, a fire "came from the Lord" (Lev 9:24; II Chron 7:1ff) and consumed the victim, it did not destroy the gift men had given but sanctified and divinized it.'[2]

Thus does virginity 'sanctify'. The privation it entails is not the sign of a destruction but of an ascension. Like the holocaust, it is an 'elevation'. Through the holocaust of virginity, man's life is sanctified and divinized. Imbued with the radiance of the divine presence, burnt by the fire of divine charity, man sees his deepest urge and power turn into an act of love for God, as the victim was turned into smoke 'to ascend' into the divine glory. Man's vital energy is sacrificed, that is, not cut off but consecrated and transfigured. In terms of modern psychology, it is sublimated. But whereas psychology, when speaking of sublimation, refers to an effort of self-purification, the sublimation of Christian celibacy is of a theological order: it means assumption; it denotes primarily the action of God accepting man's offering and lifting it up to himself. This sublimation is the work of the divine love, consuming body and soul, apparently destroying but really assuming and transmuting their longings.

This transforming holocaust is nothing else than the individual application of the sacrificial exaltation of Christ. The epistle to the Hebrews makes of this exaltation one of its leading themes: as the High Priest of old entered the Holy of Holies with the blood of the victims, Christ, with the blood

[1] R. de Vaux, *op. cit.*, p. 342.
[2] F. X. Durrwell, *The Resurrection*, London 1960, p. 62.

of his own sacrifice, entered the sanctuary of the divine presence where he sits forever at the right hand of God (Heb 9:7-12; 10:12). Supremely efficacious, done 'once for all' (Heb 7:27; 9:12; 10:10), that sacrifice is unique and its results last eternally. The significance of Christian virginity can be stated in the same terms. It is a sacrifice; united with the sacrifice of Christ, it shares in its efficacy. Virginal life consists in a total surrender to the Godward thrust contained in Jesus' sacrifice, the thrust of the 'eternal spirit' (Heb 9:14) and of generous love (Heb 10:10). This thrust snatches man away from the world to take him to the divine presence. Hence virginity reaches God or, rather, God takes it to himself; following Christ, it enters heaven and sits at the right hand of God:

'It dwells in heaven with the Father of Spirits, joining in the chorus and the dances of the heavenly Powers . . .: it gives man wings of desire to soar up to heaven; it constitutes a bond of intimacy between man and God; it is the intermediary that unites and brings together two beings, naturally so distant.'[1]

There is more than Oriental grandiloquence in that description of virginity dancing in heaven along with the angels. It is a correct appraisal of the greatness of Christian celibacy. Whereas the continence of the Old Testament, in proportion to the cult with which it was connected, was imperfect, inefficacious and could only express the hope of a better 'sanctification', hence had only a tentative character and had to be repeatedly but briefly performed, Christian celibacy has the perfection of the sacrifice of Christ of which it is a part. Like it, it is efficacious: on the part of man, it represents the absolutely radical surrender

[1]St Gregory of Nyssa, *De Virginitate* 2, *PG* 46, 324.

of the whole self to God; on the part of God, it means total acceptance of that 'living holocaust' received in the presence of the divine glory.[1] Hence, in proportion to the better cult to which it belongs, it has a decisive and lasting character: it is also done 'once for all' and never withdrawn.[2] Like Christ in heaven, it stands as a 'perfect cult to the living God' (Heb 9:14), a liturgy in which God himself is the devouring fire (Heb 12:29).

In the previous chapter, it was shown that, with martyrdom, Christian celibacy is the most radical way of embodying the νέκρωσις of Jesus, of sharing in his death.

But the death of Jesus leads to the glory of his resurrection. It was a sacrifice; that is, besides the immolation, an exaltation and a consecration. In that respect also, Christian celibacy is assimilation to the death of Christ. The sacrifice of Jesus is reproduced in the celibate when his flesh and soul are not only immolated but also exalted, made sacred, holy.

'I sanctify myself', Jesus said in the Sacerdotal Prayer

[1] It is even an antecedant acceptance since it is the divine grace, the charisma, which makes the self-surrender possible.

[2] Though Protestantism does not reject the idea of a dedicated celibacy, it does object in general to the vow of virginity. Such a pledge would amount to presumption, substituting man's self-reliance for the unpredictable ways of God's grace: 'It may be that some will live chastely outside marriage for a time, but in that we must not determine anything and take no assurance for the morrow' (Calvin, *Commentaires sur le Nouveau Testament*, Toulouse ed. 1894, III, p. 297; quoted by M. Thurian, *op. cit.*, p. 109). But this objection overlooks the lasting character of God's grace: cf M. Thurian, *ibid.* What gives virginity its perpetuity is God's acceptance of the sacrifice and not man's goodwill. Once he has accepted the sacrifice, God, who is faithful, does not withdraw his acceptance. It is by virtue of that antecedent divine acceptance and not on account of human earnestness that the sacrificial dedication is efficacious and irreversible. Ultimately the reliance of the virgin rests on the efficacy of the sacrifice of Christ: like it and in it, it is done 'once for all', it is lasting and final.

(Jn 17:19). By these words, he described his imminent death as a consecration which, while immolating his earthly existence, would lift him up to the full communion of the divine holiness. Comparing this saying of Jesus with a similar phrase of the hermetic literature, C. K. Barrett comments: 'Here (in the hermetic text) apotheosis or something of the kind is in mind; and though apotheosis strictly understood is foreign to John's thought, the present passage looks in the same direction'.[1] Christian virginity too looks in the same direction. It also is a kind of apotheosis. As Christ 'sanctifies himself', he 'sanctifies' also those who follow him, setting them apart from the world (17:15f), taking them into the divine life (17:23), in the midst of the divine glory (17:24), in the fire of the divine love (17:26). Virginity, like martyrdom, is full participation in that 'sanctification'. It is a holy life because it is, in the full sense of the term, a sacrificial life. An immolation and an exaltation, it soars, in Christ, into the divine sphere.

In the words of M. Olier, the French divine of the seventeenth century:

'A chaste soul is a soul which is risen in spirit and shares in the very nature of the risen Christ . . . It has access with him to his perfect holiness and his divine qualities which change its deepest attitude and give it the very same longings and feelings which animate the Son of God in his risen condition.'[2]

This is exactly what St Paul meant when he described virginity as a 'holy' life. It is a life assumed in God, a life in which, as far as can be at present, the sacrificial consecration and apotheosis of Christ has been fulfilled.

[1]*The Gospel according to St John*, London 1955, p. 417.
[2]*Introduction à la Vie et aux Vertus Chrétiennes*, Paris 1657, pp. 313f.

III

The Spiritual Value
of Virginity

After having inquired into the meaning of virginity in relation to the future mystery of the eschatological fulfilment, and the past mystery of the Lord's death and resurrection, it remains now to study it in reference to present-day Christian life, along the lines of what Fr Bouyer has called 'supernatural anthropology'.[1] What has virginity to do with the world we live in ? What is its place in the new life which has been imparted to the Christian ? What is its role in the life of the Church ? In other words, in what relation does man, through virginity, stand with the world, God and the Church ?

[1]"That is, the theology of man and of his destiny in the eyes of God', in *Woman and Man with God*, London 1960, p. viii.

87

Here again, Paul and Luke will be our guides. In his plea for virginity in I Cor 7, St Paul writes:

> *I would have you free from care. Now the unmarried man cares for the things of the Lord: his aim is to please the Lord. But the married man cares for worldly things: his aim is to please his wife and he is divided.*
>
> *And the unmarried woman or the virgin cares for the things of the Lord: her aim is to be holy both in body and in spirit. But the married woman cares for worldly things: her aim is to please her husband. (I Cor 7:32-34)*

Detachment from the world, complete self-surrender to the Lord, sanctity of life: those are the reasons for which Paul prefers virginity to married life. The previous chapter has explained the 'holiness' of virginity. The other two reasons which, in the eyes of Paul, make for the superiority of continence, described precisely the situation of the Christian celibate towards the world and God. They will be the object of the next two chapters. Then we shall go back to Luke to study the role of virginity in the growth of the Church.

CHAPTER FIVE

Virginity and Liberty

THE LANGUAGE of the Apostle seems plain enough: celibacy is good because it is carefree. The celibate is ἀμέριμνος, literally 'careless'. It goes without saying that this 'careless-ness' is not that of the inveterate bachelor for whom celibacy means only selfishness, attachment to comfort, privacy, aloofness and dryness of heart. Paul makes it clear that what he extols is dedicated celibacy. Worldly worries are set aside for a singleness of purpose in the spiritual life which would be impossible in marriage. But is this explanation as satis-factory as it seems? A. Robertson and A. Plummer see a striking parallel to Paul's exhortation to virginity, in the saying of Epictectus:

> Is it not fit that the philosopher should without any distraction be employed only on the ministration of God, not tied down to the common duties of mankind, nor entangled in the ordinary relations of life?[1]

This parallel raises a problem. If the parallelism of thought is real, is it not compromising for Paul? Does it not make of the Apostle, at least in this instance, a Stoic philosopher rather than a disciple of Jesus, and of virginity an inheritance of Hellenism rather than a genuine element of Christianity?

[1]*Dissertationes* 3, 22, quoted by A. Robertson-A. Plummer, *op. cit.*, p. 158.

Towards the end of Old Testament times and the beginning of the Christian era, the main trends of Hellenistic thought, deeply marked by Platonic influence, saw an opposition between matter and spirit, between the present temporal condition and the ideal world to which God and the eternal reality of things belonged. The body was considered to be a prison from which man had to escape in order that he might soar through knowledge and contemplation into the serene sphere of immutable eternity. An ideal of continent life would have fitted the logic of that system. Actually it did not develop in Hellenism as, on almost similar premises, it did in the Hindu system of the *âshramas* and in Buddhist monasticism.[1] In fact, the full consequences of the Greek dualism were drawn only by such Christian heretics as the Gnostics, Encratites, Donatists, Cathari, Albigenses and the like. They condemned marriage as unclean and made of celibacy the necessary condition for salvation. But they were heretics. The Church never condemned matrimony. Following the biblical view of the world, Christian thought cannot accept Hellenistic dualism. The material world is a creation of God; hence it is good and, in particular, the human body with all its functions is good. The order 'to increase and multiply' was given by the Creator himself (Gen 1:28) and, in the New Covenant, marriage has even been raised to the dignity of a sacrament (Eph 5:25-32).

---

[1]Yet, there were a few Stoic and Neoplatonic philosophers who considered celibacy as a higher state of life. Cf Epictectus, *loc. cit.* and *ibid.*, 3, 26f. See A. Oepke, art. γυνή in *TWNT* I, p. 779. But those views never resulted in a wide movement, creating special institutions, as was the case in India. The *âshramas* are the four stages through which, according to Hinduism, man's life should pass. After a first stage of initiation or discipleship during his youth, man marries and founds a family. Then he withdraws from the world to become a hermit. Finally giving up everything and severing every human tie, he becomes a wandering monk (*samnyasîn*).

90

St Paul does not condemn marriage in I Cor 7; yet is he not influenced by Hellenistic thought when praising virginity? What does he mean by the 'freedom from worldly cares' which virginity makes possible? Does he mean that indifference towards and disengagement from the material world which the philosophers advocated? Is his meaning not closer to the Stoic *ataraxia* or Neoplatonic *ekstasis* than to the Christian *agapê*?

Before attributing the arguments of Paul in I Cor 7 to Hellenistic infiltrations, it must be observed that such an explanation runs counter to the general trend of Paul's thought and life. Paul did not consider salvation and the Christian life as an escape from concrete realities. He had experienced ecstasy but, like all the genuine Christian mystics, he was more disturbed by it than proud of it.[1] If he mentions his raptures, it is only to prove that he has a personal knowledge of what the charismatic Corinthians used to boast of. But as for himself, he would not glory in such things: his only pride is in his share in the humiliations of the Cross (II Cor 12:1-10).

Ecstasy and deliverance from the material world were not Paul's ideal. His soul took easily to contemplation; yet he did not make of disengaged mysticism his supreme goal. His life was surely not carefree in the sense that he had nothing to do but meditate on unseen realities, for was he not the missionary who had to carry 'the daily burden, the worry for all the churches', besides 'the labours, exertions and persecutions' endured in carrying out his apostolate (II Cor 11:23-27)? When he gave himself as an example of celibate life, it was not a model of carelessness that he set up: 'Who is

[1] Cf C. Baumgarter, art. 'Extase' in *Dictionnaire de Spiritualité* IV, 2, Paris 1961, col. 2187ff.

weak and I am not weak? Who is scandalized and I am not on fire?' (II Cor 11:29). Those were not the words nor the attitude of a man indifferent to daily realities, lost in a nirvana of complete abstraction.

It is therefore *a priori* unlikely that the freedom from care which St Paul saw in virginity had anything to do with philosophical detachment from the material world. He does consider married life, which is entangled with the world, to be opposed to celibacy, which is concerned solely with the Lord. But does this contrast correspond to the Greek opposition of matter and spirit, ὕλη and νοῦς?

The answer must be negative. The biblical antithesis between the world (or the flesh) and God (or the Spirit) cannot be reduced to the philosophical dualism of matter and spirit. In the Bible, the opposition of the world to God is not ontological but moral: the world is not estranged from God by essence but by choice. Between the world and God there stands not a contradiction but a revolt. Such is the clear teaching of the first chapters of Genesis. It is true that, on account of man's sin, the whole order of the cosmos has been shaken: suffering and death have entered the world in the wake of sin. Yet though deeply marked by the curse of sin, the cosmos is not evil in itself: the trouble is in the heart of men, not in things.[1] For centuries, the prophets strove for the restoration of the original order through conversion: if only man would repent, he would recover 'life', which is the harmony and peace of the original plan. When man proved too stubborn, the prophets understood that he was doomed. Sin was too deeply engrained in the world; death had to do its

---

[1]'For evil comes not out of the earth
nor does distress spring out of the ground
But man himself begets misery
as sparks fly upwards.' (Job 5:6f)

work; the present world with all its institutions had to be taken away. Yet, since God is the God of mercy, hope remained. But it turned into the hope of a new creation, of a salvation beyond death (Is 51:6; 65:17-20; 66:22; Ez 37:1-14). It is this expectation of a world to come that the New Testament inherited. But this 'world to come' or rather 'the age to come', according to the exact meaning of the Hebrew phrase, is not the ethereal sphere of 'ideas'. Salvation does not consist in escaping the material world but in passing from one world to another, from 'this age' ruined by sin and enslaved by the 'powers' (Gal 4:3), to the 'age to come', animated by the power of God's Spirit and irradiated with the divine glory. The aim of life is not an 'ecstasy' that would snatch man out of his body and lift him above matter and outside time; it is an Exodus that raises him, body and soul, above the present condition and the corruption of sin. The image of the Exodus was frequent in the later prophets (Is 41:17ff; 43:19f; 52:11f) and passed to the New Testament (I Cor 10:1-11; Heb 2:1-4; 3:1-3; Apoc 15:1-5). Christian life is a pilgrimage (I Pet 2:11). The Christian is a refugee running from a doomed city to a place of shelter. Yet what he flees is not the flow of time but the contagion of sin, and his refuge is not his spiritual self but God's kingdom.

These were Paul's views also and they constitute the background of his apology for virginity. He does not oppose marriage and continence as matter and spirit, good and evil. What he does contrast is the age to come and the present age. Virginity embodies the spirit of the Kingdom;[1] marriage is rather an institution of this world.

As St Paul sees it in I Cor 7, matrimony belongs to the 'things of this world'. It is not a bad thing but it is intimately

[1] Cf Ch 2 above.

connected with the present transient order. It shares in the inconsistency of this order: and like the latter, it is 'subject to vanity', 'enslaved to the corruption' that marks everything belonging to the present era (Rom 8:2of). The world and its spirit are deeply engrained in matrimony: they enter married life through the very duty for husband and wife 'to please' each other (I Cor 7:33f).

The verb 'to please' in this context has a very strong meaning[1] and Paul's thought cannot be grasped properly unless this meaning is recognized. For the modern reader, the words 'to please one's husband or wife' evoke merely the show of affection and feelings and, possibly, of coquetry which expresses and fosters conjugal love. Consequently, when the text goes on to say that the married man 'is divided' (v. 33), we think spontaneously of a heart divided in its affections, in the modern romantic sense of the term. The difficulty for the married man would be that two different objects, Christ and his wife, appeal to his heart and that therefore he would be in the awkward position of being unable to give his love fully to either. This would be a very shallow explanation that hardly does justice to the views of the Apostle. After all, the love of God is not a matter of sensitivity; it belongs to a higher level and does not conflict with natural human feelings. God does not stand as a rival to his creatures, if they do not try to usurp his place. The danger in wedlock does not arise from a normal attachment of the affections to the partner; it lies elsewhere. The real meaning of the verb 'to please' points in

---

[1]The Greek verb ἀρέσκω may be very strong. Its connotations are not merely sentimental. In I Cor 10:33, Paul's desire 'to please everybody' does not mean that he aims at popularity or that he avoids hurting the feelings of others. It expresses Paul's readiness to oblige, almost to serve all. It means about the same as 'being all to all' (I Cor 9:22). Cf W. Förster in *TWNT* I, p. 455.

another direction. In a world which had little concern for chivalry and romanticism,[1] more than coquetry and a show of affection was required 'to please'. The wife 'pleased' her husband by giving him the children he wanted (and birth control was not unknown in the Greco-Roman Antiquity)[2] and by conducting the household efficiently (with the con-

---

[1] Cf J. Carcopino, *Daily Life in Ancient Rome* (Penguin ed., 1956), pp. 94f; W. J. Woodhouse, art. 'Marriage (Greek)', in *ERE* VIII p. 444.

[2] Cf A. E. Crawley, art. 'Foeticide' in *ERE* VI, pp. 55ff. Child exposure also was not uncommon. Polybius attributed the decline of Greece to the ὀλιγανθρωπία caused by those practices: 'In our times the whole of Hellas has been afflicted with a low birth rate or, in other words, with depopulation, through which the states have been emptied of inhabitants with an accompanying fall of productivity—and this in spite of the fact that we have not suffered from any continuous wars or epidemics ... The people of Hellas had entered upon the false path of ostentation, avarice and laziness and were therefore becoming unwilling to marry, or if they did marry, to bring up the children born to them; the majority were only willing to bring up at most one or two, in order to leave them wealthy and spoil them in their childhood; and in consequence of all this the evil has been rapidly spreading. Where there are families of one or two children, of whom war claims one and disease the other for its victim, it is an evident and inevitable consequence that households should be left desolate and that states, precisely like beehives, should gradually lose their reserves and sink into impotence' (Polybius, *Hist.*, xxxvi, 7, quoted in A. J. Toynbee, *Greek Civilization and Character*, New York 1953, p. 73). Modern authors have confirmed the judgment of the old historian: 'The misery of a few districts in the third and second centuries BC would not suffice to explain the excesses of malthusianism; indeed it had always been a part of Greek manners but at that time it took frightening proportions. Though we should be cautious in giving a general value to a few figures known only through epigraphy, they are not without significance. At Miletus, for 79 families which received the citizenship between 228 and 200, we find only 146 children, out of which 28 girls only; among those 79 families, 31 have two children and 32 only one. In the course of the third century, at Eretria, one out of twelve families, and at Pharsalus one out of seven, has more than one son; out of 600 families known through the inscriptions of Delphi, six only have two girls. Seeing that, we cannot doubt the accuracy of the famous statement of Poseidippos: "Even a rich man has once exposed a daughter" ' (R. Cohen, *La Grèce et l'Hellénisation du Monde Antique*, Paris 1948, p. 580).

cessions to the ways of the world which efficiency involved).[1] For the husband, it was a matter of securing for his wife wealth, comfort and social consideration. 'Pleasing' each other covered all aspects of the conjugal life, everything that made a marriage successful. It is easy to understand that such worldly success implied all sorts of compromises with the spirit of the world. Through the desire 'to please', the 'worries of the world' (v. 33) entered married life, those worries which, according to the parable, combined with wealth and pleasures, choke the growth of God's Word (cf Lk 8:14).

If St Paul is reticent with regard to marriage, it is not because marriage distracts the heart but because it tends to sink deep roots into the present age of sin. Those roots are so deep that it is very difficult to cut oneself free, to preserve in wedlock the soul of a pilgrim and to live the Exodus. Conjugal affection is not contradictorily opposed to Christian requirements but the danger is great of remaining bogged down in the present condition, of considering pleasure, family welfare and honour as the absolute goal, of letting matrimony degenerate into a mere worldly affair. What one would attempt if one were alone, one dare not do for the sake of the other so that actually, through the other party, it is the world and its spirit which enter the family. Conjugal harmony is preserved at the cost of condescensions to the weakness found or supposed to exist in the other. It is harder in wedlock than in single life to behave in this life as a citizen of heaven, to follow the ideal of the Beatitudes, to be poor and meek, to bear persecutions happily, to accept being

[1]See the rather blunt statement of the Pseudo-Demosthenes (59, 122): 'We have heterae for our pleasure, concubines for the daily care of the body and wives to beget legitimate children and to have somebody who can be trusted with the care of the household.'

hungry and downtrodden. How rare the spiritual harmony that enables a whole household to meet the challenge of the Kingdom joyfully! As Bacon said, 'he that hath wife and children hath given hostages to fortune' and 'children sweeten labours but they make misfortunes more bitter'.[1]

It may be said that this picture of matrimony is one-sided, that Christian matrimony is not only 'a thing of this world'. It also has reference to the world to come by its sacramental value. This is true and the point will be considered later.[2] It is clear that, to give a complete and balanced theological appraisal of matrimony, Paul should have said that it is in the measure in which it is not transformed by the divine *agapé* that conjugal love divides the soul. He should have explained that for husband and wife the desire to please each other is wrong only if, and as far as, they represent for each other not Christ but the world with its devious judgments and seductions.

But in I Cor 7, Paul does not intend to give a full theology of marriage. Either because he still needed to appreciate fully the positive Christian value of matrimony, or simply because—as he often does—he simplifies his thought to express it more clearly, he considers only the 'worldly' aspect of married life. This worldly aspect does exist. For all its sacramental value, marriage is partly bound up with the present times. It must have this worldly side to be a sacrament at all, to be a sign. And there is always a risk that it is only this aspect that will be seen by men and that they will set their heart on the sign instead of reaching out to what is signified. Sacramental realities can also be veils. Thus, when eating manna in the desert, or the miraculous loaves of

[1] Quoted by A. Robertson-A. Plummer, *op. cit.*, p. 154.
[2] See pp. 104-107.

7

Jesus, the Jews considered only 'the food that perisheth' (Jn 6:27) and dreamt of an earthly kingdom with an unlimited and effortless supply of bread. They failed to perceive in the bread the power of God's Word feeding them unto the 'life of the age to come' (Jn 6:26-40). Thus, as experience proves, married people are easily tempted to set their heart upon the present tenor of marriage and lose sight of its sacramental dimension. In I Cor 7, Paul referred to that common experience which had taught the Corinthians that married life is not easily a clear and limpid reflection of the divine *agapê*. Concretely the necessity for husband and wife 'to please' each other often entails compromises with the world for, as St Paul and his Christians knew well, it is hardly possible 'to please' both man and Christ (Gal 1:10).

This is the significance of the contrast Paul saw between marriage and virginity. Marriage is rooted in this world. Virginity belongs to the age to come.

Marriage is not condemned. It does not necessarily embody the evil of this world: it can be redeemed and transfigured. Yet it is discouraged. This is not because it multiplies earthly obligations and petty worries restricting the mental freedom to meditate and contemplate. Neither is it because it proposes objects of affection other than Christ. It is not wife and children which disturb men but their worldly requirements, real or supposed. The danger of matrimony is that, by the whole force of circumstances which surround it, it tends to remain a 'thing of this age' and to enfold men in the spirit of this world.

By contrast, virginity is the ideal condition of the pilgrim who wants to progress swiftly and unencumbered across the desert. Lightly shod and with loins girt, he goes on his

Exodus; he leaves the world behind and strives after the world to come.

He is undivided. This does not mean that he has feelings of affection for no one but Christ. On the contrary, his love for Christ will have to take on the dimensions of the whole Body of Christ and will have to encompass the world. It means that no human love, no necessity 'to please' man, will oblige him to side with this world and place him under the tension of one who belongs to both sides and is torn between two loyalties and two spirits.

He is free: he has no cares, at least no cares pertaining to this world. He does not know the concerns which settled family life is almost bound to cause, concerns for wealth, comfort, safety, fame. He has not the problem of securing welfare and tranquillity for his dear ones in a world which has lost its balance. The Christian celibate has none of these worries. This again does not mean that he has no cares at all and that he has nothing else to do but devote himself to intellectual and ascetical pursuits. He has his cares, the 'cares for the things of the Lord' (vv. 32, 34).

'The things of the Lord' which should be the virgin's only concern are not the suprasensible ideas attained by contemplation. The 'Lord' in St Paul is the risen Christ, endowed with power and glory after his resurrection.[1] 'The things of the Lord' are therefore the whole order which has the risen Christ as its centre, the New Creation, the Kingdom and, here on earth, the Church.[2] As in the case of the

---

[1]'This designation expresses as does no other the thought that Christ is exalted to God's right hand, glorified and now intercedes for us before the Father' (O. Cullmann, *The Christology of the New Testament*, London 1959, p. 195). Cf also the several studies of L. Cerfaux gathered in *Recueil Lucien Cerfaux*, I, Gembloux 1954, pp. 3-188.

[2]The Vulgate and the Latin Fathers have 'idealized' the opposition

Apostle himself, the concern for the 'things of the Lord' will not mean *ataraxia*, indifference. The Christian celibate will not be spared the heavy burden and the burning pre-occupations of his service to the Lord. But they will be only the outward manifestation of his devotion to his Master (cf I Cor 9:19).

Such is the freedom of the virgin. It is not the indifference which is reflected, for instance, on the serene features of the gods of Phidias, with their clear eyes that ignore the turmoil of the world to rest on the harmony of the changeless ideas. We could rather feature the Christian dedicated to virginity as the Moses of Michelangelo (without the gigantism which is the artist's own): there is no indifference in him: he looks firmly at the children of Israel who surround him and his eyes reflect the love of God for the chosen people but also the divine disappointment and wrath. Beyond them, he sees the Holy Land—or the mountain—whither he must lead them. His muscular body strains towards it; his face glows with the glory that dawns upon it.

between marriage and virginity by reading in v. 32 *quomodo placeat Deo* (instead of Κυρίῳ of the Greek text) and probably understanding similarly, in v. 34, *Domini* of God instead of Christ (as Knox has done in his translation). By doing this, they bring the contrast closer to Platonic thought. For Paul, the contrast is not directly between the world and God, creatures and Creator, but between the world and the 'things of Christ', that is between the present world and the New Creation which Christ contains in himself.

CHAPTER SIX

Virginity and Charity

THE TYPOLOGY of the Exodus does not entirely cover the reality of Christian life. At the same time as it is an Exodus, Christian life is also life in the Land of Promise. We are still in the desert; yet already the glory of the new Jerusalem dawns upon us. We are still in the flesh and in the world; yet already we live in Spirit and are citizens of heaven (Phil 3:20).

Correspondingly, virginity belongs not only to the desert but also to the new Jerusalem. It shows not only the tenseness of the pilgrim who wants to be unimpeded in his progression, but marks also the joy of arrival, when the soul has at last found what it longed for. Celibacy is not only total detachment from 'the things that are upon the earth'; it is also total communion in 'the things that are above'. It is life, 'hidden in God with Christ' (Col 3:1-3). Free from the world, the celibate ties himself to Christ with bonds of love. Having no wife or husband 'to please', the celibate is at liberty to dedicate all his care 'to please the Lord' (I Cor 7:32).

Here also, when St Paul says that the aim of the virgin is 'to please the Lord', we should beware of giving the phrase a merely sentimental significance. 'To please the Lord' does not mean simply to comfort and console the Heart of Jesus.

In our context, 'to please the Lord' is set in parallelism with 'to please his wife'. This parallelism invites us to give the same strong meaning in both cases. In the context of matrimony, the verb 'to please' expressed the interdependence and mutual belonging of husband and wife. When applied to the celibate, it must describe the loving enslavement to Christ which gives continence its value. The virgin belongs to Christ as the wife belongs to her husband. To please her husband, the wife must entirely share in his views and wishes. By analogy, to please the Lord, the virgin must be totally dedicated to him and adopt his viewpoint in everything. The theme of spiritual marriage lies in the background. The construction of the whole passage points to that theme: by balancing in parallelism virginal life and conjugal union, Paul suggests that, in a certain way, Christ is to the virgin what the husband is to the wife.[1]

The theme of spiritual marriage figures explicitly and is connected with virginity in II Cor 11:2.

> I am jealous for you with a divine jealousy. For I betrothed you to one husband that I may present you as a chaste virgin to Christ.

[1] Cf X. Léon-Dufour, 'Mariage et Continence selon St Paul' in *A la Rencontre de Dieu, Mémorial Albert Gelin*, Le Puy. Paris 1961, pp. 322-324. In a penetrating literary analysis of I Cor 7, the author shows that the very construction of the chapter expresses the mutual belonging of virginity and matrimony. The chapter is built on a scheme ABA' (two corresponding parts divided by a digression), quite common in Paul's epistles. Part A (vv. 1-16) is addressed to married people and part A' (vv. 25-40) to the unmarried. Now we notice that in both parts the progression of the thought is disturbed by considerations belonging to the antithetic section: A speaks already about virginity (vv. 6f) and A' cannot but evoke matrimony 'as if the continence to which Paul invites his flock could be given its full significance only in relation to married life' (p. 323). Thus, 'the very literary and psychological trend of the chapter shows marriage and continence as two inseparable realities contrasting with and yet completing each other' (p. 324).

This verse is a short allegory comparing the Corinthians to a betrothed girl taken to the bridegroom by her father or by the *mesitês*, the go-between who arranged the marriage. The image derives from the Old Testament where Israel is frequently called the bride of Yahweh (cf Os 2:21f; Jl 1:8; Is 54:5f; 62:5; Jer 3:1; Ez 16:6-43). Admittedly this text does not refer directly to the question of virginity. As in the Old Testament, the bride is not an individual but a community; here, the church of Corinth. Moreover the marriage it alludes to will be celebrated only at the Parousia; for the time being, the Church is only 'betrothed'. In that context, 'virginity is nothing else than a metaphor expressing undivided dedication to Christ.'[1] Yet it is not insignificant that Paul uses the comparison of a 'chaste virgin' to describe the union of the Church with Christ. It implies that virginal life is a living likeness of that union. What was a mere metaphor in the Old Testament takes flesh and blood in the person of the virgin. She embodies fully the mutual belonging of Christ and the Church. The 'marriage feast' of the Parousia is anticipated in her life. She is given to live in all its integrity the undivided attachment of the Church for her Head. In her shines the *agapê* which joins the bride to the bridegroom and makes them 'one body'. Virginity is *agapê*: it has all the intensity of love; it is not primarily disengagement and withdrawal. It is unqualified dedication to the 'one husband', Christ. It shows forth the exclusiveness of that unique attachment. As St Paul says, using the language of human passion, it is a 'jealousy', a love impatient of any alien allegiance.

Christian virginity is a spiritual marriage with Christ. It is true that Paul himself did not use the phrase. Neither did Luke when explaining the relationship of the Virgin Mary

[1] G. Delling, *TWNT* V, p. 835.

with the Holy Spirit in the Gospel of the Infancy. The reason is probably that Paul and Luke spontaneously avoided words which, in the world they lived in, were too heavily loaded with pagan connotations. The ἱερὸς γάμος, the sacred union of a god with a woman, had been a common feature of mythology from Sumerian times onwards and had its ritual representation in the cult and in the mysteries. In the framework of nature worship or of a pantheistic religion, it symbolized the fecundity of nature. There is obviously no relation between the pagan fertility cults and the Christian ideal of continence followed by Mary and the virgins. And it is understandable that Paul and Luke refrained from using the phrase 'spiritual or divine marriage' that would have been too easily misunderstood as another case of ἱερὸς γάμος. That their prudence was justified is proved by the wild conclusions which the comparative school of exegesis, from the times of Celsus till our own day, has drawn from the discreet allusions they made to the biblical theme of God's alliance with Israel.

Yet it is the allegory of marriage, stripped of any association with nature worship, which accounts best for the Pauline and Christian doctrine of virginity. The doctrine of virginity branches off from the doctrine of matrimony. We must therefore see what marriage meant for Paul in order to understand what 'spiritual marriage' might have meant for him had he used the words, and what he had actually in mind when he wrote of 'the chaste virgin presented to the one husband Christ'. It is in Eph 5:25-32 that the Apostle explains most fully the Christian significance of matrimony. It can be said that, if I Cor 7 pictured wedlock as in fact it is, Eph 5:25-32 shows it in all its ideal sacramental beauty. But the 'lofty sacrament' opens on to the prospect of virginity.

In Eph 5:25-32 as in II Cor 11:2, the Church is compared to

the bride taken to the bridegroom for the nuptial celebration:

> Husbands, love your wife as Christ loved the Church: for her, he gave himself up, sanctifying her, cleansing her by water and word, so that he might present the Church to himself all glorious, with no stain or wrinkle or anything of the sort but holy and without blemish. Thus men should love their wives.

In this text, there is no go-between: Christ himself prepares his bride and there is a stress on the point that she was not pure but was made so by the cleansing love of the divine Spouse. That love which cleanses in the laver of baptism springs forth from the cross: the words 'saviour' and 'he gave himself up' show the sacrificial background of Paul's thought. The cross was already the marriage function which II Cor 11:2 had seen within the setting of the Parousia. It is on Calvary that the bride, cleansed by the love of her Spouse, was embraced by him to become 'one body' with him.

The greatness of Christian matrimony derives from its relation to the union of Christ with the Church which was realized on the cross. Conjugal love, that mysterious power which tears man and woman away from their families to draw them together (v. 31), was a sign, a 'mystery'. It had a hidden significance. In a secret way, it prefigured the love, the *agapê* that seals together Christ and the Church and makes them one body (v. 32). The Old Testament did not know this mysterious orientation of the conjugal union but now the mystery is revealed. If placed under the influence of the sacrifice of Christ, that is, if lived in the spirit of unselfishness and dedication which inspired the sacrifice of Christ, conjugal love symbolizes the bond of charity which unites the Church with her Head and contains the life flowing through their joint Body (vv. 23, 30). Penetrated with the Spirit of

Christ, matrimony enshrines the divine *agapê*; it continues the sacrifice of Calvary and its efficacy. By that sacramental efficacy and in the line of that symbolism, each party represents for the other Christ and his requirements of self-denying charity: husbands love their wives as Christ loved the Church and wives obey their husbands with the same joyful submission which animates the Church (vv. 33, 22-25). In the measure in which conjugal affection becomes charity, wedlock is holy and 'has a relevance to Christ and the Church' (v. 32): indeed it is a part of their mysterious union.

Now, 'lofty' as it may be, the 'mystery' of Christian matrimony remains a sign, as imperfect and inadequate as any sign. After all, in Eph 5:25-32, it is not said that Christ loved the Church as a husband loves his wife, but rather that husbands should love like Christ. Conjugal love does not explain the union of Christ with the Church; on the contrary this union reveals the latent signification of marriage. The *agapê* of Christ is set as the ideal norm of human love: it is the reality, whereas matrimony is only its sacrament.

Though the 'mystery' it contained has been revealed, matrimony keeps its existence and its consistency of sign, as if the veil had not been removed but only pierced by a powerful light. The light shines through, the veil becomes the medium of communication of light; but it is still there and, transparent as it may be, it may still absorb some of the light. Containing a significance and an efficacy pertaining to the world to come, matrimony keeps its earthly solidity and persists in its 'this-worldly' existence. At the same time as it announces the eschatological marriage feast of the Lamb, it remains union in a flesh not yet transfigured by the Spirit.[1]

[1] The point can be expressed technically in theological language which, in the sacraments, distinguishes between the *sacramentum tantum*, the *res*

We saw that it is that 'worldly' aspect of matrimony which is responsible for its spiritual opacity.[1] The spiritual reality may be absorbed in the worldly density of the 'sign' and, even in the most favourable cases, when it is at its most transparent, matrimony remains a sign, a reflection, not the light itself. This sacramental value of matrimony is both its greatness and its imperfection: the 'mystery' is at once revealed through the screen, yet hidden in its worldly folds. Or, to take an image of Paul's, it reflects the *agapê* of the cross, but only in the cloudy and confused manner of the old mirrors of polished metal (cf I Cor 13:12).

Because it is a closer participation in the sacrifice of the cross, virginity represents better the *agapê* which animated it. It not only reflects that love, it embodies it. Virginity is not a sacrament. It does not set the screen of any sign between Christ and man. In it, the divine love is not refracted through the mediation of any worldly feeling. There is nobody who stands for Christ, to represent him: the contact between Christ and the bride is direct. Matrimony turned towards the *agapê* of the sacrificed Christ as towards its fulfilment; virginity shares directly in that *agapê*. The *agapê* lived in matrimony is mediated charity; virginity is love reaching its object directly.

In the words of the Roman Liturgy:

> While no prohibition lessens the dignity of marriage and while the nuptial blessing resting on matrimony is

tantum and the *res et sacramentum*. In matrimony, the *res* is the divine *agapê* sealing the unity of the mystical Body as it seals the conjugal union. The *sacramentum tantum* is the conjugal bond. Christian marriage is *res et sacramentum*: there is intercompenetration of the symbol and of the spiritual reality. Christian virginity on the contrary is the *res tantum* of matrimony.

[1] Cf p. 97f.

107

safeguarded, nevertheless there will be nobler souls who, spurning the carnal union entered by man and wife, strive after the mystery it represents (*fastidirent connubium, concupiscerent sacramentum*). Without imitating what takes place in matrimony, they devote their entire love to the mystery signified by marriage (*nec imitarentur quod nuptiis agitur, sed diligerent quod nuptiis praenotatur*).[1]

Virginity is plenitude of *agapê:* it shows forth the reality which matrimony contains in only a veiled way. It is the full revelation of the 'mystery' still half hidden in sacramental marriage.[2]

Like the love of the Spouse in the Canticle, the *agapê* of the Christian celibate is 'a blazing fire, a flame of Yahweh' (Cant 8:6).[3] This fire of love makes of virginal life a holocaust in which the 'flesh' is burnt up and with it any sign, any reality of the present world. Virginity is love impatient of the mediation of any symbols. In that respect, too, it is analogous to the sacrifice of the cross: the death on the cross was a sacrifice without rites because, in its utter despoliation, all the symbolical realities of the world came to an end; there remained only the naked corpse on the bare wood, in a total holocaust of everything belonging to this world. Virginity, too, is a feast without rites, a marriage banquet celebrated without any external rejoicings because, as on the cross, this marriage is consummated and consumed in a

---

[1] *Preface of the Consecration of Virgins* in the Roman Pontifical. We follow the translation given in L. Munster, *Christ in his Consecrated Virgins*, Collegeville 1957, pp. 131f.

[2] 'To be living images of the perfect integrity which forms the bond of union between the Church and her divine bridegroom is assuredly the supreme glory of the virgins' (Encyclical letter *Sacra Virginitas*, *AAS* 26 (1954), p. 173).

[3] We follow for this text the translation of A. Robert, *Le Cantique des Cantiques* (*BJ*) Paris 1951, p. 58.

holocaust of self-denying love that raises it above this world.

It is in that sense that virginity is a spiritual marriage. It is a *marriage*: in the phrase 'spiritual marriage', the adjective does not obliterate the noun. Virginity is love, total communion with the divine *agapé* which is the essence of the life of Christ and of life in Christ.

This marriage is *spiritual*. Spiritual does not mean metaphorical. The spiritual union of Christ with the virgin is not a vague likeness of the conjugal union. It is rather the opposite: virginity gives the true picture of real love in all its intensity and purity.

Neither is it spiritual in the Platonic sense of the term. It does not correspond to any chimerical dream of abolishing the body. In virginity the body is accepted as it was in the Incarnation. But it is sanctified, transformed as the flesh of Jesus was in his glorification. The glorification does not delete the Incarnation: it fulfils it. Virginity is no negation of the flesh but its consecration.

The virginal union with Christ is spiritual in the biblical sense of the term. It shows man's transformation by the power of the Spirit. The Spirit, the divine force that animates the New Creation, takes possession of man's body and soul, freeing them from 'the shackles of corruption' to give them 'the glorious liberty of the children of God'. And the transforming force which the Spirit implants in the virgin is the charity of God (Rom 5:5), the flame of love which, coming from God, consumes the flesh of the virgin and transmutes it into the likeness of the 'spiritual flesh' of the risen Christ (I Cor 15:45-49).

The New Testament does not explicitly call virginity a spiritual marriage. Yet its doctrine of marriage and its exhortations to virginity converge towards that theme, because both states of life refer to the mysterious connubial union of Christ and the Church which marriage prefigures and virginity embodies. Linked by that common relation to the mystery of Christ, virginity and matrimony are intimately connected. Matrimony moves towards a virginal type of love as towards its fulfilment and virginity is nothing but the full realization of that which is prefigured in marriage.

The best exposition of the spiritual meaning of Christian virginity would be therefore a Christian exposition of the Canticle of Canticles, the nuptial song of the Old Testament.[1]

The Liturgy, the Fathers of the Church and the mystics have understood this spontaneously and have repeatedly made of the Canticle the epithalamium of the Christian life dedicated to the Lord.

Drawing from Origen's *Homiles on the Canticle*, the *Commentary* of St Bernard and the *Spiritual Canticle* of St John of the Cross, it would be easy to compose a magnificent anthology in which the best of Christian eloquence and lyricism would figure. As a sample of what this anthology would contain, it is difficult to resist the temptation of quoting at least extracts of the hymn with which Methodius concludes his *Symposium on Chastity*. The ten virgins who have taken part in the *Symposium* conclude their discussion with the triumphal chorus:

> For Thee, I keep myself chaste,
> and with a lighted torch in hand,
> O my Spouse, I come to meet Thee.

[1]Such transposition is not too distant from the literal sense if it is accepted that in its literal sense the Canticle is an allegory of the Covenant relationship of Yahweh with Israel. Cf A. Robert, *op. cit.*, pp. 7-23; A. Feuillet, *Le Cantique des Cantiques*, Paris 1953.

And these stanzas follow, composed by Thecla, the most eloquent of the ten:

> From above, O virgins, there came the sound of a voice that raises the dead. It says: Hasten to meet the Bridegroom in white robes and with lamp in hand. Turn to the East. Arise lest the King should precede you at the gates.
>
> For Thee, I keep myself . . .
>
> For Thee, O King, spurning a rich home and the embrace of mortals, I came in spotless robes, to enter with Thee within the bridal chambers.
>
> For Thee, I keep myself . . .
>
> In my eagerness for Thy grace, O Lord, I forget my own country, I forget the dances of my companions, the desire even of my mother and kindred, for Thou, O Christ, art all to me.
>
> For Thee, I keep myself . . .
>
> O blessed Bride of God, thy couch do we adorn with hymns. And we praise Thee, O Church, immaculate virgin, pure like snow, wise, undefiled, lovely.
>
> For Thee, I keep myself . . .
>
> Open thy gates, O resplendent Queen and take us too within the bridal room. O spotless and triumphant Bride, breathing beauty, behold we stand round Christ, clad like Him, singing thy nuptials, O happy maiden.[1]

The canticle of Methodius weaves a web of biblical themes. The bride of the Canticle and of Ps 45 has joined the bridegroom of the parable (Mt 25:1-13). The voice that rouses the ten virgins is that which has called Abraham and invited him to leave 'home and kindred' for the first Exodus

[1] *PG* 18, 208f. A substantial part of the hymn is quoted and translated by E. J. Quasten, *Patrology* II, Utrecht 1953, pp. 130f.

to Canaan (Gen 12:1). It is also the voice that raised Christ from the dead. The nuptial procession is at the same time an Exodus and an Ascension that takes the Church and the virgins to the bridal chamber of the King. There is more in that text than fanciful allegory: the profusion of biblical allusions shows a thought deeply rooted in biblical ground. The hymn echoes Paul's call to virginity. Though amplified, the exhortation of the Apostle is rendered faithfully. The attitude and the bliss of the ten virgins corresponds exactly to the ideal proposed, by Paul to the Corinthians, of a life 'free from worldly worries' to be spent 'waiting upon the Lord without distraction' (I Cor 7:35).

CHAPTER SEVEN

Virginal Fecundity

THE AIM of virginity is not to suppress the conjugal union but to fulfil it. It must therefore realize conjugal fecundity also. Being a spiritual marriage, it must have also a spiritual fecundity.

It had this fecundity in the case of Mary, the mother of the Saviour. Obviously her fecundity was a unique privilege granted her in view of the role she had to play in the plan of salvation. Yet does it not contain a universal value?

Commentators have often pointed to the parallelism of Luke's Gospel of the Infancy with the beginning of the Acts of the Apostles: the same starting point in Jerusalem, the same emphasis on the work of the Spirit accompanied by numerous charismatic manifestations, the same atmosphere of joy expressed through hymns and canticles, the same multiplication of angelic interventions. There can be no doubt that, when narrating the beginning of Jesus' life, Luke perceived in it the dawn of salvation and the advent of the Kingdom, of the New Creation wrought by the Holy Ghost. We are therefore entitled to look in those chapters for a theology of the 'new man' and in Mary's virginity for teaching on the significance of Christian virginity.

It is understood that the Infancy Gospels have nothing

8

to do with the literary form of parenesis. Their aim is not to make the 'book of the origins of Jesus Christ' (Mt 1:1) a call to chastity and a panegyric of virginity. 'By the very intention of the author, we must take a theological standpoint and not that of an invitation to temperance (chastity-virginity): we deal with events by which all benefit rather than with the merits of an individual and the personal favours bestowed upon her.'[1]

This is quite true and our intention is to keep to the theological standpoint. In accordance with the intention of the evangelists, our aim is to determine the significance of Mary's virginity, and of Christian virginity in general, within the framework of the new economy. If it is true that, beyond the individual case narrated by the evangelists, their interest reaches Christian life at large, it is likely that they saw in the fecundity of the Virgin an event of universal import and it is a legitimate search that attempts to retrace this significance.

1. *The Spirit*

Mary's miraculous motherhood is the work of the Spirit: such is the teaching of the Infancy Gospels of Mt and Lk which, for all their circumstantial divergences, agree at least on the basic truth of Jesus' virginal and 'spiritual' begetting (Mt 1:18; Lk 1:34f). Now how did they understand the intervention of the Spirit at the Incarnation?

Matthew does not tell much about it. The begetting by the Spirit is mentioned only casually, as a well known fact which needs no comment. At most we might point to a certain stress on the word γένεσις (origin) (1:1, 18). In v. 18, the use of the word is all the more striking for being unexpected:

[1] J. P. Audet, 'L'Annonce à Marie' in *RB* 63 (1956), p. 349.

it is rather γέννησις (begetting) that should be used,[1] and quite a number of Mss do not hesitate to bring in the correction.[2] This must be an influence from the book of Genesis: Mt 1:1 begins the Gospel with the very words of Gen 2:4 βίβλος γενέσεως). Hence it might be inferred that Mt attributed to the Spirit in the 'genesis' of Christ the same role the Spirit had 'at the beginning' in the 'genesis of heaven and earth'. In that case, Jesus' begetting by the Spirit in Mt 1:18 would correspond to the creative work of the Spirit in Gen 1:2; the birth of Christ would mark the advent of the new heaven and new earth, of the new creation announced by the prophets (Is 43:18f; 67:17). This interpretation is quite likely. Yet it cannot be denied that the text touches but lightly on that theme. The point of the account lies elsewhere.

The text of Lk fortunately has a clearer theological slant. Lk 1:35, particularly, surrounds the intervention of the Holy Ghost with a collection of themes which may help to determine the significance of the work of the Spirit. Yet there have been many different interpretations of this verse.[3]

[1]See W. C. Allen, *The Gospel according to St Matthew* (*ICC*), Edinburgh 1912, p. 9.
[2]Mostly the Mss depending on the Syro-byzantine recension (K family) and already Ireneus and Origen. M.-J. Lagrange (*Evangile selon St Matthieu*, Paris 1948, p. 8) prefers the reading γέννησις but commentators on the whole do not follow him. We can apply here the principle: *lectio difficilior potior*.
[3]See particularly R. Laurentin, *op. cit.*, which gives (pp. 191-223) a rich bibliography on the question. Several recent studies have compared Lk 1:35 with the verse of Ex (40:35 in the LXX) which describes the coming of God's glory on the Tabernacle. In both texts, the Greek verb ἐπισκιάζειν refers to the divine presence. This verb, rendering the Hebrew *shâkan*, evokes the theme of the *Shekinah*, the indwelling of God among men and in Christ, the Sanctuary of the New Covenant (Jn 1:14). There is much in this suggestion. Yet it does not cast much light on the problem we are studying here, for the typology of the Temple has little to do with the role of the Spirit. In the Bible, the theme of the Spirit does not seem to have much connection with that of the Temple.

The comparative study of religions would like to compare Jesus' virginal conception to the pagan narratives of theogamy or at least to see in it an infiltration through the Gospels of those scabrous legends narrating the love-affairs of the gods with their earthly mates. Quite fashionable in the heyday of the *Religionsgeschichtliche Methode*, this view, which is still patronized by R. Bultmann,[1] has been refuted many a time. To put it briefly in the terms of C. K. Barrett:

> The cases . . . of the semi-divine begetting of individuals by a god and a woman have no contact with the Matthean and Lucan stories at the point where we are concerned with them, namely, the statement that the conception of Jesus was due not to an act of paternity on the part of a god but to the supernatural and non-material action of the Holy Spirit.[2]

If many authors look in pagan Hellenism for an explanation of Jesus' virginal conception, it is because, they say, the Judaism of New Testament times knew nothing like the creative role attributed to the Spirit by Matthew and Luke in Jesus' birth. Frequent in the Old Testament (Gen 1:2; Ps 33:6; 104:30; 147:18; Job 27:3; 32:8; 33:4; Prov 8:22ff; Ez 37:1-14; Is 44:3f), the idea of a creating Spirit would be foreign to old rabbinical literature.[3]

Thus, for the rabbinical commentaries or the targumim of Gen 1:2, the *ruah* hovering over the waters at the beginning was either simply the wind or allegorically the spirit of Adam

---

[1] *Theology of the New Testament* I, London 1952, p. 131.
[2] *The Holy Spirit and the Gospel Tradition*, London 1947, p. 8.
[3] Cf *Str.-Bil.* I, p. 48.

or of the Messias.[1] The Spirit was considered only as the instrument of prophetic revelation or as the moral power inspiring the just.[2] At Qumran also, the Spirit has mostly ethic connotations.[3]

Yet there were exceptions. *Str.-Bil.* mentions Jdt 16:14 and Apoc. Bar. 21:4. Other texts can be quoted that refer to the power of the Spirit to re-create and restore life in the days of the Messias.[4] Wis 7:22-27 too should go on record: a text not too distant from the New Testament times, it describes Wisdom identified with the Spirit (vv. 22, 25), renewing everything (v. 27), an obvious allusion to Ps 104:30. The idea of a vivifying and creative Spirit was not altogether unknown in Judaism. Even if it does not occur often in the writings of the Rabbis, it may have kept all its vitality among the people.[5]

In New Testament times, the great biblical texts on the role of the Holy Ghost in the New Creation were still read

[1]Such is not the case with the newly discovered Neofiti Targum for which the *ruah* of Gen 1:2 is 'the Spirit of love coming from Yahweh'. Even the *ruah*-wind of Gen 8:1 becomes for this Targum 'a spirit of love' (*ruah de rahamin*).

[2]Cf E. Sjöberg in *TWNT* VI, pp. 384f (English translation in *Spirit of God*, London 1960, pp. 7-14); C. K. Barrett, *op. cit.*, p. 21.

[3]Cf E. Schweizer in *TWNT* VI, pp. 387ff (Eng. tr. in *op. cit.*, pp. 15-18); W. Förster, 'Der Heilige Geist im Spätjudentum' in *NTS* 8 (1962), pp. 122-134.

[4]'God said to Israel: In this world my Spirit has put Wisdom in you, but in the future my Spirit will make you to live again, as it is said, I will put my Spirit in you that you may live, Ez 37:14' (*Ex. Rabba* 48, 102d; cf *Gen. Rabba* 96, 60d) quoted by C. K. Barrett, *op. cit.*, p. 21.

[5]Thus, among the frescoes of the synagogue of Dura-Europos on the Euphrates, there was a representation of the vision of the dry bones in Ez 37. These paintings belong only to the third century AD but they would have followed old standard patterns: cf C. H. Kraeling, *The Excavations at Dura-Europos, Final Report VIII, Part I, The Synagogue*, New Haven 1956, pp. 385-402.

and meditated upon. The vision of the dry bones in Ez 37 for instance is often quoted (by the Apocalypse especially: 11:11= Ez 37:5, 10; 20:4= Ez 37:1-14; 21:3= Ez 37:27; and also by St Paul: I Thess 4:8= Ez 37:14; II Cor 6:16= Ez 37:27).[1] The early Church knew the texts referring to the activity of the Spirit in the last days and proposed them to the reflection of the faithful. St Paul in particular sets the New Creation in the Spirit among the leading themes of his theology. Rom 8 is an elaborate description of the work of the Spirit reviving the world in the person of the risen Christ and of the Christians who live in him:

> If the Spirit of him who raised Jesus from the dead dwells within you, the God who raised Christ Jesus from the dead will also give new life to your mortal bodies through his indwelling Spirit (Rom 8:11).

Christian life—and first of all the life of the risen Christ—is 'pneumatic', life in the Spirit and from the Spirit (I Cor 15:44-50). The resurrection is the fulfilment of Ezechiel's prophecy: put to death in the person of Jesus, Israel comes under the influence of the Spirit and leaves the tomb to live for ever a transfigured life. From the life of the flesh, Jesus— and mankind in him—pass for ever to the life according to the Spirit. The power of the Spirit works in them a transforming regeneration (Rom 8:14). Thus, by the action of the Holy Ghost, the risen Christ becomes the 'first born' of the New Creation (Rom 8:29; Col 1:18; Heb 1:6; cf Apoc 1:5). To live in him means having access to the καινὴ κτίσις (II Cor 5:17; Gal 6:15; Eph 2:15; 4:24), the new world entirely animated by the impulses of the Spirit.

[1]Concerning the relations between the Apocalypse and Ezechiel, see M. E. Boismard, *L'Apocalypse* (*BJ*), Paris 1950, p. 14.

Luke, Paul's disciple and the evangelist of the Spirit, could not but have these overtones of the theme of the Spirit in mind when he related the begetting of Jesus. There is no need to search elsewhere for the theological background against which he and his readers set the action of the Holy Spirit at the beginning of Jesus' life. In line with the most genuine biblical tradition, Luke saw in Jesus' begetting the work of the Spirit as Creator. The Spirit that came upon Mary to give life to the Son of God was the Spirit who was to restore to life the dry bones of Israel. It was also the Spirit who would inaugurate the New World through the Resurrection. By recalling his part in the Incarnation, Luke traced to the very beginnings of Jesus' life the theology of the New Adam and of the New Creation which Paul and the Early Church had contemplated in the glory of the Resurrection.

Luke perceived a deep analogy between the Incarnation and the Resurrection: for him, both are due to the creative power of the Spirit. This analogy can best be brought out by a comparison between Lk 1:35 and a passage of the prologue of Rom (1:3f). The parallelism is so close that the two texts can be written synoptically, each key term of the verse of Luke finding a correspondence in the words of the prologue.[1] Both texts hinge on the same themes: divine sonship, power, holiness and the Spirit. The analogy appears still more clearly when it is noticed that the context too is similar,

---

[1]

Rom 1:4	Lk 1:35
Constituted *Son of God*	The *Holy Spirit* will come upon thee
in *power*	and the *power* of the Most High will cover thee
according to the *Spirit of Holiness*	this is why the *holy* child to be born will be called *Son of God*.

since in Rom (1:3) as in Lk (1:32) it refers to Jesus' Davidic lineage. In Lk as in Rom, the mystery of Jesus is stated in terms of a dual human and divine lineage, of the race of David and of the Spirit, and both authors explain the part of the Spirit in similar terms.

The similarity is too great to be dismissed as casual. The conclusion follows that, when relating the Annunciation, Luke was influenced by the Pauline formula or, rather, by the old confession of faith which Rom 1:3f embodied. To narrate Jesus' origins, Luke followed a tradition which, as we find also in Mt 1:18, referred to the role of the Holy Spirit. This mention of the Spirit was enough to set in motion the association of ideas in the mind of the evangelist. He let the terms of the well known formula of faith seep into the tradition which he followed. It is indeed typical of Luke's manner lightly to touch up a text so as to bring out its theological implications: Luke was an expert in that art.[1]

Doing this, Luke transferred to the conception of Jesus what Paul had connected with the Resurrection. For Paul and the Early Church, the Spirit was the principle of life of the age to come. Because it was the work of the πνεῦμα ζωοποιοῦν, the Resurrection was the beginning of that age. Breathing life into the body of Christ and the Church united with this body, the Spirit inaugurated the world to come and made it a present reality of which the 'first fruits' (Rom 8:23), the 'first instalments' (II Cor 5:5; 1:22) are already given to us. It is the same πνεῦμα which Luke saw at work in the begetting of the New Adam and in the new Genesis. In 1:35, Luke transfers to the Incarnation the view of faith which his predecessors had perceived in the Resurrection. From the very day of the Incarnation, the vivifying Spirit was active

[1] Cf E. Osty, *L'Evangile selon St Luc* (*BJ*), Paris 1948, pp. 10-24.

and realized in Jesus the eschatological transformation of mankind. Thus, with the coming of Christ into the world, the last times have started. The Spirit is given and breathes a new life. In Jesus, he creates mankind anew, brings to existence a new race which has access to the life of God's children, is free from the yoke of the devil and is animated by the divine δύναμις. Jesus leads the way in this new life (Ac 3:15); he is the Head from which flows the life he has first received. Begotten by the Spirit, shaped by him, Jesus is the starting-point of the new world where it is no longer the flesh and its sorrows that prevail, but the power of the Spirit and the joy of God's children.

2. *The Virgin*

What took place mysteriously in the womb of the Virgin at the Annunciation was that which appeared in its full light on the day of the Resurrection. In Jesus' conception and in his resurrection, we see the same work realized by the same Spirit. In the tomb as in the Virgin's womb, it was the πνεῦμα ζωοποιοῦν inaugurating the καινὴ κτίσις.

This analogy of the begetting with the Resurrection explains the virginity of Mary. The earthly birth of the Messias had to be virginal for the same reason that his messianic birth had to be through a resurrection from the dead. To create anew, the Spirit had to work on an annihilated flesh; the life-giving breath of God had to blow on inert matter. In Pauline theology, it is the cross that represents the total divestment of self, the κένωσις of Jesus, stripping away all power and glory according to the flesh (Phil 2:7). In Lk, it is the Virgin's womb that stands for the weakness of the flesh.

Did Luke actually perceive this analogy between Mary's virginity and the cross? He saw the Spirit as the principle of a new life and Jesus' conception as an anticipation of the Resurrection. Did he also realize that Mary's virginity was already a proleptic participation in the mystery of the death of Christ? Did he consciously make of the virgin's womb a type of the cross?

Though the idea may seem far-fetched at first, it may not have been so distant from Luke's mind.

He considered virginity as a way of sharing in the sacrifice of the cross.[1] It would not be surprising that he gave the same value to Mary's virginity.

Moreover, paschal symbolism plays a predominant part in Luke's Gospel of the Infancy. Like the Gospel itself and the narrative of the Temptation, the first two chapters of Lk are built on the pattern of the progress to Jerusalem: from the very beginning, the events of the life of the Saviour seem to be 'driven by a mystic force towards Jerusalem, the scene of the Passion and of the Triumph'.[2] The birth narrative starts from Galilee (1:26) and comes to an end in Jerusalem, more precisely in the Temple, where the child appears both as 'a sign of contradiction' and as 'the light for the enlightenment of the nations' (2:32, 34). Is not this already the paschal paradox of rejection and glorification? Then the infancy narrative takes Jesus again to Galilee (2:39) to bring him once more to the Temple of Jerusalem, and during the course of a paschal feast (2:42) he disappears to be found again on the third day 'with his Father' (2:49).[3] It would be

[1] Cf Ch 3 above.
[2] E. Osty, *op. cit.*, p. 18. Concerning the allusions to the paschal events in Lk 1-2, see R. Laurentin, *op. cit.*, pp. 15, 31f.
[3] See discussion of this text and bibliography in R. Laurentin, *op. cit.*, p. 143.

quite surprising if Luke and his readers should have failed to notice in these facts a prefiguration of the last Passover. Like the Temptation in the desert (Lk 4:13), the Infancy Gospel is an anticipation of the καιρός, of the time appointed by divine dispensation for the fulfilment of the plan of salvation. If it is true that a paschal typology underlies the Infancy Gospel and if, for Luke, virginity is a sharing in the Passion, it becomes highly probable, to say the least, that Luke saw the cross outlined against the mystery of Mary's fecund virginity. This virginal fecundity announces the life-giving death of the Redeemer. Like the cross, the Virgin represents the weakness of the flesh made strong by the action of the vivifying Spirit. The association of the Virgin with the Spirit is the Lucan correspondence to the anti-thesis 'flesh-Spirit' in Paul.

Is this supposing too much Paulinism in Luke? Even if this were so, and if it were wrong to find so much explicit theological reflection in the text of Lk 1-2, it would at least remain true that—even independently of any Pauline influence and of any relation to the theme of the flesh—Mary's virginity, in Luke's Gospel of the Infancy, means poverty and powerlessness.

This is clearly the meaning of the Magnificat. In its context, in relation to Elizabeth's greetings (Lk 1:43), the Magnificat is the joyful song of the young mother thanking God for the supernatural offspring she has been given. As in Ps 113, the mother rejoices over her child, all the more so since the child is the Messias (1:32f), the Son of God (1:35), the Lord (1:43).

To describe the miracle of this fecundity, the canticle develops the contrast of God's wonderful deeds with the lowliness of his handmaid. Verse after verse, it sets forth the paradox of a poverty made rich, of misery turned into happiness. In the context of a thanksgiving hymn sung by a young mother, the wonderful deed can be nothing else than the miraculous begetting that has taken place in her. By contrast, the 'lowliness', the low estate—we could almost say the humiliation[1]—of the handmaid can only be that of her being a virgin, deprived of the joys of motherhood. Mary's ταπείνωσις in 1:48 balances the ὄνειδος, the disgrace which Elizabeth considers to be attached to her sterility in 1:25.

This interpretation is confirmed by the fact that the Magnificat follows closely the canticle of Anna in the book of Samuel (Lk 1:46= I Sam 2:1; Lk 1:48= I Sam 1:11; Lk 1:51= I Sam 2:7; Lk 1:53= I Sam 2:5). In the text of the LXX, Anna uses the word ταπείνωσις to describe her condition (I Sam 1:11; 2:7) and it is clear that in her case her wretchedness comes from being barren. Mary borrows the terminology of Anna: she compares herself to Samuel's mother. Her 'humiliation' is the same as Anna's: it is the humiliation of having no child. As a true Jewess, she does not consider virginity as a quality, a meritorious condition, but as a privation, a mean condition.[2]

Thus, according to the Magnificat, Mary's virginity is the humiliation that has been removed, the cause of contempt which is replaced by universal admiration (1:48) the want that has been turned into riches (1:52). For the Infancy Gospel, Mary's maidenhood is therefore utter poverty, lack not only of earthly goods but of the very quality which gave a woman a title to self-esteem and to the respect of others.

---

[1] The Greek word ταπείνωσις is one of the strongest terms used by the Old Testament to mean poverty. It does not mean humility but humiliation, and corresponds almost always to the Hebrew 'oni: distress, wretchedness.
[2] Cf p. 19ff.

Hence the coming of the Spirit upon Mary will be the encounter of God with the poor; it will be a case of the divine power choosing to work on 'what the world counts weakness . . . thinks low and contemptible, mere nothings' (I Cor 1:27f). This corresponds to a constant law of divine action. God's power has a marked preference for the poor and the weak. The Old Testament in its entirety is regulated by that law of the strength of the weak, the fecundity of the barren, the election of the poor. Ultimately this law finds its highest application in the 'scandal of the cross', this 'divine weakness stronger than men' (I Cor 1:23, 25).

Now we can understand the exact value of Mary's virginity. Its value is analogous to that of the death of Jesus. In the theology of the Infancy Gospel—even if Luke was not positively aware of the similitude—Mary's virginity plays the role the Cross has in Paul's synthesis. The ταπείνωσις of the Virgin receives all its significance from its relationship to the ἐταπείνωσεν of Calvary (Phil 2:7). Mary's virginity is not good in itself, for in itself it is nothing but abasement. As the death of Christ would be nothing without the Resurrection, Mary's virginity, for the evangelist, would come to nothing, would be mere wretchedness, without the life giving power of the Spirit.

3. *Fecundity according to the Spirit*

The Virgin and the Spirit evoke respectively the cross and the glory. In Mary's womb as in the tomb, the divine power brought forth from the weakness of the flesh the first-born of the New Creation. When narrating the Annunciation, Luke did not intend to tell of a prodigy but to describe the dawn of the regenerated world. Mary's virginal motherhood is not only miraculous: it is 'spiritual'. Being the work of the Spirit, it marks the beginning of the age of the Spirit and of life in the Spirit. Born from Mary, the child will be a son of David and of Adam but also, because of his divine and spiritual begetting, he will be animated by a new life and will be a son of God.

This is what the angel goes on to explain to Mary in Lk 1:35b, after he has told her of the coming of the Spirit upon her: 'That is why (διὸ καὶ), he says, the holy child to be born will be called Son of God.'

This text is difficult. How are we to explain that διὸ? How is Jesus' divine sonship linked with the role of the Holy Spirit in the Incarnation? We submit that the theology sketched in this study may lead to a solution of this vexed problem.[1]

Usually commentators understand Jesus' divine sonship in Lk 1:35 of the eternal sonship of the Word in the bosom of the Trinity. On this assumption, it is rather hard to explain how the way the Incarnation took place in time can have anything to do with the eternal relation of the Son with the Father.

For some, the text would mean that the virginal birth will make Jesus *known* as the Son of God.[2] But the text does not say that. Others would translate καὶ by 'also': the miraculous birth of Jesus would be only an additional reason—and a minor one—why Jesus is called Son of God.[3] But to defend this interpretation, we have to stretch Greek grammar—and also logic—to the breaking-point. Another translation would be

[1] A full survey of the question may be found in A. Médebielle, art. 'Annonciation' in *SDBV* I, col. 275-278; 290-294.
[2] 'διὸ explicari debet de causa cognitionis Filii Dei': J. Knabenbauer, *Evangelium secundum Lucam*, Paris 1896, p. 71.
[3] Cf P. Bover, 'Quod nascetur (ex te) sanctum vocabitur Filius Dei', Lk 1:35, in *Biblica* I (1920), p. 94.

'that is why the child to be born will be called holy, Son of God'. Those who favour this interpretation suggest that the διό bears directly on the first predicate, on the special holiness of the child, the second predicate depending only in a loose manner.[1] But this translation has not much to commend it and moreover it is rather difficult to suppose that, out of two predicates depending on the same conjunction, one should do so strictly and the other only vaguely.

Fr S. Lyonnet's explanation offers the advantage of taking the words at their face value and of keeping clear of grammatical and logical acrobatics. The verb ἐπισκιάζειν (overshadow) in Lk 1:35 evokes the theme of the *Shekinah*, of the divine presence in the Tabernacle and the Temple. Gabriel's choice of this term amounts to a description of Mary's womb as 'the Tabernacle of God, the only place on earth where God was going to live' and *that is why* 'the child to be born must be the Son of God, not a divine being only but God himself',[2] since he will be the manifestation in the flesh of God's presence. This would be a satisfactory explanation if we could accept that the whole text hinges on the verb ἐπισκιάζειν and that this allusion to the theme of the *Shekinah* gives the key to the understanding of the whole passage.[3] But is this not giving too much importance to an allusion? The actual text of Lk 1:35 explicitly puts forward a group of themes which definitely belong to the core of Luke's message. Is it wise to overlook his central thoughts and focus the explanation on the possible implications of an allusion?

[1] A. Médebielle, *art. cit.*, col. 292ff.
[2] S. Lyonnet, 'Le Récit de l'Annonciation et la Maternité Divine de la Sainte Vierge', in *Ami du Clergé* 66 (1956), pp. 45f.
[3] See the qualifications P. Benoit adds to his appreciation of R. Laurentin's work in *RB* 63 (1958), pp. 45f.

There is no need to do away with the obvious sense of Lk 1:35. The text does say that it is because he was born from the Spirit that Jesus is the Son of God. It follows that Jesus' divine sonship referred to in this text cannot be the eternal and ontological Trinitarian sonship of the Word. As Lagrange has it in the conclusion of his study of this verse: 'Rather than stretching the text too much, it is better to recognize that it does not give a complete doctrine of the Incarnation.'[1] But, if Lk 1:35 does not use the term Son of God in its ontological sense, what does it mean?

If there is any weight in our suggestion that the wording of Lk 1:35 was to some extent influenced by the confession of faith underlying Rom 1:3f, it can be said that, in the message of the Annunciation, Jesus is given the title of Son of God in the sense it had in the old formula. In Rom 1:4, this confession of faith shows Jesus 'set up Son of God in power through the resurrection from the dead'. This cannot refer directly to Jesus' divinity. It is in his humanity that Christ, through his exaltation, receives the divine dignity which was his when he pre-existed in God before his coming into the world (v. 3). Henceforth, his humanity will be the Temple of

---

[1] *L'Evangile selon St Luc*, Paris 1948, p. 36. It goes without saying that the soteriological meaning of the title of Son of God, as we propose it for Lk 1:35, does not exhaust its significance. It is obvious that this title, not only in Jn but also in the synoptists (Mt 11:27; Lk 10:22) has overtones which evoke an ontological and transcendent relation of Christ with the Father. In the New Testament, still more than in the Old, the implications of the title Son of God are very broad. Between the merely moral sense (Wis 18:13) and the definitely ontological meaning, there is place for a whole range of meanings. Each text must be studied in its own context to find out its precise connotations. It is highly probable that Luke, a disciple of Paul, understood that the temporal sonship of Jesus was deeply rooted in his eternal sonship. Yet this awareness was only in the background: the wording and the immediate intention of the author did not reach so far.

the Divinity, will be filled with divine power, irradiating divine glory (cf Phil 2:5-9). It is the man Jesus who, by his resurrection, enters the new order of the Spirit, becomes 'pneumatic', divine. It was with a similar thought in mind that St Peter had spoken of Jesus being 'made Lord and Christ' at his resurrection (Ac 2:36). By colouring the dialogue of the Annunciation with the themes of the old confession of faith, Luke retraced to the beginning of Jesus' life the divine investiture of the Messias. By his virginal, or rather 'spiritual' birth, Jesus was son of God—not indeed in an ontological and eternal but in a concrete and soteriological sense. Imbued with the Spirit from his very conception, Jesus was in a hidden way, from the very beginnings, that which the action of the Spirit would bring to full light at the Glorification. In his humanity, he was the Son of God, the human bearer of the divine power and glory.

Jn 1:12f may be another text which sees a direct relationship between Jesus' supernatural origin and his soteriological divine sonship.

The interpretation of the text depends on the solution which is given to a problem of textual criticism.

The standard text reads: 'He gave the power to be called children of God to them that believe in his name, who were born not of blood nor of the will of the flesh nor of the will of man but of God.'

But it appears from several old witnesses of the text that at least some sections of the Early Church read '. . . to those that believe in the name of Him who is born not of blood nor of the will of the flesh etc . . .'.[1] If this reading is chosen,

---

[1]These witnesses are: for the *Vet. Lat.*, the *Codex Veronensis* and the *Liber Comicus*; for the Syriac versions, several MSS. of the Peschitta and the

9

the text of John definitely refers to Jesus' supernatural origin.

It is true that this text is not attested by any Greek MS. But may we not prefer to the testimony of the MSS., most of them relatively late, the indirect witness of the earliest Christian literature? Many recent studies have shown the value of that indirect textual tradition.[1] And even if the Bodmer Papyrus (P 66) has not confirmed the patristic reading of Jn 1:13, it has nevertheless justified the interest taken in the versions and the patristic quotations since, in a survey of the Papyrus, Fr Boismard could draw a list of 49 cases in which P 66 confirms the testimony of the Fathers and the old versions against the Greek MSS.[2]

If the reading in the singular is taken, Jn 1:13 comes so close to Lk 1:35 that we may wonder whether there was any literary relation between the two texts.[3] In this case, it would be quite legitimate to look to Jn 1:13 for enlightenment on Lk 1:35. Jn 1:13 says that Jesus was born neither from the blood nor from the flesh. This means that he was not born

---

Dureton palimpsest; among the Fathers, Ireneus, Tertullian, Clement of Alexandria, Origen and possibly also Ignatius of Antioch and Justin. Cf also the *Indiculus of the Ps. Jerome* (*PL* 81, 639) quoted by J. Duplacy, *Où en est la Critique Textuelle du Nouveau Testament?*, Paris 1959, p. 52, n. 238.

[1] M. E. Boismard, 'Critique Textuelle et Citations Patristiques' in *RB* 57 (1950), pp. 401-408 and *Le Prologue de St Jean*, Paris 1953, pp. 56-65 (English trans. London 1957); F. M. Braun, 'Qui ex Deo natus est (Jean 1:13)' in *Aux Sources de la Tradition chrétienne, Mélanges offerts à M. Maurice Goguel*, Paris 1950, pp. 11ff and *La Mère des Fidèles, Essai de Théologie Johannique*, Tournai-Paris, 1954, pp. 33-38. See however the opposite view of A. Houssiau, 'Le Milieu Théologique de la Leçon ἐγεννήθη dans Jo 1:13' in *Sacra Pagina, Miscellanea Biblica Congressus Internationalis Catholici de Re Biblica* II, Paris-Gembloux 1959, pp. 170-188.

[2] *Le Papyrus Bodmer II*, in *RB* 64 (1957), pp. 391ff.

[3] F. M. Braun, *La Mère des Fidèles*, p. 29 thinks that there was a reciprocal dependence. Such is also, for the two Gospels of Lk and Jn in general, the opinion of D. Mollat, *L'Evangile et les Epîtres de St Jean* (*BJ*), Paris 1953, p. 39.

by a merely natural birth, that his birth is not the result of man's initiative and power. Even if the clause 'nor by the will of man' is not genuine,[1] it constitutes at least an old and accurate assessment of the meaning of the preceding words.

Jesus was 'born of a woman': the evangelist would not give the lie to Paul's statement (Gal 4:4). Indeed he insists repeatedly on the fact that Mary was Jesus' mother (2:1, 3, 5, 12; 19:25f). This birth shows how fully the Word became flesh. Yet, human and real as it may have been, this birth is not a birth according to the flesh. The mother of the Saviour was a virgin: that is, according to the laws of human fertility, she was unable to bring forth. That Jesus was born of that inability shows that his birth belongs to another order of fecundity. It must be remembered that, according to the Hebrew mind, the role of women in the conception of children was merely passive. The initiative came from man: it was the man who 'took' a woman, 'went' to her, 'knew' her. The subject of those stock phrases in Hebrew is always man and this reveals an outlook which supposed that man alone was active. Also, when the child was born, it was the father's 'name' which he revived (cf II Sam 14:7; Dt 25:5-10), the father's 'house' he made firm, the father's lineage he continued.[2]

A virginal birth was therefore a birth in the flesh, but neither from the flesh nor for the flesh. It was a birth situated outside the framework of any human lineage, the birth of one whose family and home were out of this world.

Such was Jesus: he was not born to continue any worldly family but to head the line of God's children. The name he bears is not the name of a human family. He was the son of

[1] Cf M. E. Boismard, art. cit., p. 405.
[2] Cf J. Pedersen, op. cit., pp. 68-74.

Abraham, but this was immaterial in comparison with his divine origin (Jn 8:33-38, 53-58). Born of a virgin, without any active human principle of generation, he was born of God: he came from above (Jn 3:31). If 'he that is of the earth is earthly' (Jn 3:31), he is not earthly. He is 'spirit' in the biblical sense of the word: he belongs—belongs pre-eminently—to the regenerated sphere of the Spirit (cf Jn 6:53-63). For he is born of the Spirit and 'he that is born of the Spirit is spirit' (Jn 3:6).

At the conception of Jesus, the active principle of generation was the Spirit and, to beget him, the Spirit acted as Spirit. His intervention was not theogamic: it was not carnal but properly 'spiritual'. Because the principle was the Spirit, the outcome also was spiritual; born of the Spirit, the child was the bearer of the Spirit. Born in the flesh, he did not belong to it: the weakness of his flesh shone with the glory of the Son of God and his humanity was the temple of that glory (Jn 1:14).

In Lk 1:35 and, if we accept the patristic reading, in Jn 1:13, Jesus is given the title of Son of God in the sense that he is the one who first and *par excellence*—other texts will make it clear that it was by right of eternal generation—receives the divine life in his humanity. His flesh becomes the Tabernacle of God and is the abode of the Father's power, glory and wisdom, thus becoming the source of life for those who believe in him and receive him. The virginal conception takes its value from that context. Wrought in the flesh but not by the power of the flesh, the virginal birth belongs to a unique sphere. According to the flesh, the womb that bore Jesus was inert. In Mary, human fecundity had reached total renouncement; in return, the Spirit created in it a new order of fecundity that transcended nature's aspirations, achievements and limitations. In the Virgin, human fecundity acknowledges its weakness and withdraws; the fecundity of the Spirit takes its place. It is more than a miracle; it is a new stage in the economy of salvation. The old order of the flesh gives place to the new life in the Spirit; a new world begins and life in the Spirit invades the flesh. This life is a divine life: it is beyond flesh and blood and no human generation can communicate it. For man is born to it 'from above' (Jn 3:3) by receiving the gift of the Holy Ghost. It was to bring that new life to the flesh that the Spirit came upon Mary and the glory of Mary consisted in her entire surrender to that new life.[1]

[1]'The Holy Ghost came upon Mary . . . This is why what was born is holy and Son of the Most High God, the Father of all, who brought about the Incarnation and manifested the new generation, so that we might inherit life through this generation, as we had inherited death through the former one . . . And this is why, in the end, not by the will of the flesh, nor by the will of man, but by the good will of the Father, his hands have restored life to men, so that Adam might turn into the likeness and similitude of God.' Commenting upon this text of St Ireneus (*Adv. Haer.* v, 1, 3), A. Houssiau concludes: 'The allusion to Jo 1:13 is ambiguous or rather bivalent; the text applies both to Christ and to Christians. But the interest of the author bears primarily on the anthropological problem, that is, on the spiritual generation of the believer' (*art. cit.*, pp. 180f). We think that this 'anthropological interest', without excluding the application of the text to Jesus, corresponds to the deeper sense not only of Jn 1:13 but also of Lk 1:35. In an interesting discussion, E. Hoskyns, while choosing the plural reading of Jn 1:13, shows the intimate connection which in Jn links the spiritual regeneration of the faithful and the Incarnation of the Word: it is this connection which explains the transition between vv. 12 and 14, and which would account also for the early Fathers' application of the verse to Christ: 'The Evangelist employs a phraseology actually used for or obviously suggestive of the Virgin Birth, transferring or applying it to the desired spiritual miracle of Christian regeneration, but in such a way that the reference to the miraculous birth of Jesus is preserved and presumed.' The conclusion is that 'the singular *was born* is a corruption of the text but a corruption that is neither unnatural nor unintelligent' (*The Fourth Gospel*, edited by F. N. Davey, London 1947, pp. 165f). Even if we were to accept the reading in the plural for Jn 1:13, the other reading would keep its interest

Thus it appears that Mary's virginal fecundity, though unique, was not an isolated case, a meteorite, as it were, fallen on biblical ground from some mythical sky. The mystery of her fecundity had deep roots in the history of salvation. It is the mystery towards which the Old Testament groped obscurely through all the supernatural births that steadily marked the development of the Chosen People. To do God's work the power of flesh and blood does not suffice and, to show that the history of Israel was divine work and a process of grace, the race of Abraham appears, from its very origins, as a lineage that owes its existence not to the flesh but to the Promise and the Spirit. This was already the lesson of the birth of Isaac as St Paul understood and explained it (Gal 4:22-31; Rom 4:13-17; 9:6-12). The development of the Old Testament implied that 'there were two posterities of Juda and two races, as it were two houses of Jacob: one that was born of flesh and blood, and the other of faith and of the Spirit'.[1]

Rooted in the mystery of the election of the poor, and still more in the vivifying power of the cross, the mystery of weakness and power contained in Mary's virginal mother-hood has thus a universal value. In the life of the Church it will extend to the whole world.

4. Spiritual fecundity in the Church

Prefigured in Sara and realized in Mary, the fecundity of

as a patristic confirmation in favour of the interpretation, 'neither un-natural nor unintelligent', that we propose here: behind the reference to the children of God, the Fathers would have perceived the presence and the influence of the Son of God; for them the supernatural begetting of Jesus contained the type of our spiritual regeneration.

[1] Justin, *Dial. cum Tryphone* 135, 6 (quoted by A. Houssiau, *art. cit.*, pp. 173f).

the Spirit will extend in the Church to the dimensions of the world.

The Church, too, is the sterile woman who becomes a mother (Gal 4:26f). Like Mary, the Church is the virgin who is met by the Spirit (cf Apoc 22:17) and in that encounter becomes the mother of the living, the locus of the new creation, the womb where the New Adam is born. In her, the work of the Spirit spreads through the flesh, and through the sacraments the world is transformed and passes from its carnal existence to the life of the Spirit.

This may have been the latent meaning of the episode of Mary on Calvary in John's Gospel. If it is true that the fourth Gospel 'traces the line from the Christ of history to Christ the Lord of the community in which the Word continually becomes flesh'[1] and that consequently 'the historical events (of Jesus' life) ... contain in themselves ... references to further facts of salvation with which these once-for-all-events are bound up',[2] one is entitled to see a symbol of the Church in Mary, the 'woman' associated with the work of salvation (Jn 2:1-11) and constituted mother of the disciple at the time of the Exaltation (Jn 19:25-27). Mary, united with all her faith to the abasement of Calvary, receives the Spirit, represented by the water flowing from the side of Jesus (Jn 19:34-37; cf 7:38f), to give it to the disciple and extend to him her spiritual motherhood. Similarly, the Church stands permanently with Jesus on Calvary. She shares in his dereliction and in everything which the cross stands for. Then come the waters of the Spirit upon her; they make her fecund and flowing from her through the sacraments, transform her into the mother who gives birth

[1] O. Cullmann, *Early Christian Worship*, London 1953, p. 38.
[2] *Ibid.*, p. 56.

in Christ to the New Creation. The Virgin, fully united to the anguish of the cross and receiving the gift of the Spirit, stands for the Church who continues in the world the mystery of the Passion and its vivifying power.[1]

One may hesitate to read so much symbolism into a Gospel. There is no reason to question it in the Apocalypse, which in ch 12 gives the description of a 'sign' which has much in common with the episode of Mary on Calvary, with definite reference to the theme of the spiritual motherhood (vv. 2, 5, 17).

This chapter has received many different interpretations.[2] Who is the 'woman travailing in birth', suffering and glorious, standing as a 'sign' over the present final period of the history of salvation? Is she Mary or the Church? Many would see in her only the Church. But the difficulty of such a collective interpretation is that actually the thought of the author seems to bear on the personal Christ as it appears from vv. 5 (with its allusion to Ps 2:9) and 17, where a clear distinction is made between the 'rest of the children' and the first child who can only be Jesus. And if the first child is Jesus, it is difficult to imagine that the author of Apoc spoke of his mother without thinking of Mary.

On the other hand, 'the description the author gives of the birth of the Messias corresponds in no way to the event of Bethlehem'.[3] It is not only that the sufferings of the mother cannot be reconciled with the dogma of the virginity *in partu*,

[1] On this ecclesiological interpretation of the episode of Mary on Calvary, see E. Hoskyns-F. N. Davey, *op. cit.*, p. 530; R. H. Lightfoot, *St John's Gospel*, Oxford 1956, pp. 317-320; A. Feuillet, 'Le Messie et sa Mère d'après le Chapitre XII de l'Apocalypse' in *RB* 66 (1959), p. 82.

[2] A. M. Dubarle surveys the main interpretations and their exponents in 'La Femme couronnée d'Etoiles,' in *Mélanges Bibliques rédigés en l'honneur de André Robert*, Paris (no date), p. 512.

[3] A. Feuillet, *art. cit.*, p. 58.

it is also and mostly that the apocalyptic significance of these sufferings, the atmosphere of anguish which surrounds them cannot be made to fit the joyful character of the mystery of Bethlehem.

The solution, recently proposed by A. Feuillet, consists in seeing in the woman first of all a personification of God's people, while keeping in the background a mariological perspective.[1] The pangs of birth are those of Calvary (cf Jn 16:19-22). The messianic birth is that which took place on Easter Sunday (cf Ac 13:33; Heb 1:5; 5:5), the birth of the First-born from the dead (Col 1:18; Apoc 1:5). At the beginning of the chapter (vv. 1-5), God's people, like Mary, gives birth to the Messias: this is the Gospel. Then (vv. 6, 13-17), they take refuge in the desert where, in the midst of persecutions, but strengthened by the divine protection, they expect the final consummation: this is the history of the Church.

This messianic birth fulfils the Proto-evangelium and also, as Feuillet and Cerfaux suggest,[2] the prophecy concerning

---

[1] *Ibid.*, p. 72.

[2] A. Feuillet, *art. cit.*, p. 67; L. Cerfaux-J. Cambier, *op. cit.*, pp. 103, 110-112. The LXX translation of Isaias may have been a step in that direction when it translated the *'almah* of 7:14 by παρθένος. The *'almah* of the Hebrew text hardly suggests a virgin birth; παρθένος almost certainly does. Thus the LXX text constitutes an important dogmatic development. Is it simply due to an inspired distraction of the Greek translator? Or must we have recourse to the comparative study of religions and suppose an influence of the Egyptian myths on the Alexandrian scribe who rendered the text into Greek? Another explanation is possible. The translator gave the prophecy a messianic sense. Emmanuel is the Messias; his mother, the *'almah*, is Israel, God's Spouse from which the Messias must come. Since Israel is often called 'virgin' in the Bible, the translator would have used that appellation spontaneously to render *'almah*. The mystery of a virgin birth may not have been foremost in his mind: he was rather thinking directly of the messianic fecundity of 'the Virgin, daughter of Sion'. Yet, by putting together virginity and motherhood, he gave the first hint of the mystery that would be fulfilled in Mary.

the Virgin who conceives, in Is 7:14. The very word 'sign', heading the chapter as it does, evokes the prophecy. The vision of the 'woman' refers to the mystery of the virginal fecundity announced by the prophet, but that mystery is seen through the other mystery of the cross. The fecundity of Israel—who in Mary gave birth to the Messias through the pangs of Calvary—continues through the fecundity of the persecuted Church. The whole episode bears also the features of Mary's messianic and universal motherhood. Mary's virginity, Calvary, and the persecutions of the Church appear therefore as three levels of the same mystery. At the three levels, we see the virgin daughter of Sion, forlorn and abandoned (cf Amos 5:2; Jl 1:8) who, by God's power, sees her anguish turn into hope and her sorrows into birth-pangs (cf Is 66:7ff). Thus the persecuted Church, always forsaken yet always fecund, carries on in herself the mystery of the lowliness of the Virgin and of her happy motherhood, of the 'exinanition' of the cross and of its power.

Christian virginity goes on proclaiming and showing forth to the world this same mystery. The same ch 12 of Apoc describes the martyrs associated with the mystery of life and death which animates the Church: 'By the blood of the Lamb, they have also conquered and by the witness of their martyrdom, for they have scorned life till death' (v. 11). The virgins render the same testimony (Apoc 14:4).[1] Like the martyrs, they have been given to embody fully the spiritual fecundity of the Virgin, of the cross and of the Church. They have given up the fecundity of the flesh. They refuse to put their hopes in this world, for they know that this world cannot offer them any firm hope. Like the martyrs, 'they have scorned their life', and not only their own indi-

[1] Cf Ch. 3, pp. 46ff above.

vidual life but also that kind of vicarious survival found in one's descendants. They have met the Spirit and now they know that the true fertility of the new world is that of the Spirit working in the Church, her faith and the sacraments.

Christian virginity is solitude and stripping of self. But the torments of that stripping are only the sign of the new fecundity of virgins, when they have received the visitation of the Spirit. Their daily death is a continuous begetting, and like Mary and the Church, it is the Messias they beget. Such is probably the full meaning of Jesus' words at the Last Supper:

> You shall lament and weep while the world will rejoice.
> You will be in grief but your grief will turn into joy.
> A woman in labour is in pain because her time has come
>   but when she has brought forth a child, she forgets her anguish
>   for joy that a man has been born into the world.
> So also you are now in pain; but I shall see you again
>   and your heart shall rejoice and your joy nobody will take from you (Jn 16:20ff).

This text is commonly understood as a simple comparison contrasting present sufferings with the joy that will prevail later on. There may be much more in those verses: they may give a full explanation of the fecund value of Christian suffering. They allude to the prophecies of the motherhood of Sion in Is 26:16f and 66:7ff. The sufferings of the disciples, like those of Sion, are birth-pangs.[1] The anguish of the

---

[1] R. H. Lightfoot, *op. cit.*, p. 317, suggests that this text finds its first application to Mary on Calvary (as a type of the Church); this would account for the use of the words 'hour' and 'man' (instead of child) in v. 21. The 'hour' in Jn is that of the exaltation on the Cross and, in the case of the spiritual motherhood of Mary, of the Church and of the disciple, what is born is really a 'man' and not a child, since it is the new Adam, the First-born.

disciples is the sign of their fecundity. This text should be set in parallelism with Apoc 12: both passages describe the 'sign' of the 'woman in travail'. In Apoc 12, the sign refers to the collective fate of God's people; Jn 16 applies it to individuals but, in both contexts, the same basic significance is to be found.

Like the Virgin in the Infancy Gospels and in the Apocalypse, the disciples bring forth the Messias: they beget him in themselves, or rather the Spirit begets him in them (Rom 8:9f). Made fecund by the Spirit, the faith of the disciples becomes pregnant with Christ: Christ dwells in their hearts (Eph 3:17) and becomes their life (Phil 1:21). Any Christian comes under that fecundating power of the Spirit if he shares in the death of the Master. But because dedicated celibacy is one of the most radical forms of that 'mortification' in union with the Lord, it is celibacy that absorbs most fully the work of the Spirit and shows it forth. Whereas the life of the children of God, though real and efficacious, is commonly veiled by the flesh, it shines unveiled through the transfigured flesh of virgins. By the charismatic sign of continence, the Spirit manifests more fully the depth of God's children. Christian celibacy is the charisma by which it is given to the disciple to know no other fecundity than that of the Spirit and to be its living embodiment.

To virginity the Spirit can add the charisma of apostolate, through which spiritual fecundity flows outwards and covers the world. If the dedicated disciple receives this additional grace, he will share most fully in the fecundity of the Virgin and of the Church. Participating in the divine fatherhood, he will beget new men (I Cor 4:14f; II Cor 6:13; I Thess 2:8, 11; Phm 10). Like the Apostle, in anguish and suffering, he will beget Christ in his spiritual children (Gal 4:19). But even if they do not receive formally the external charisma of apostolate, the virgins share mysteriously by their very virginity in the fecundity of the Spirit. For Christ who is born in their hearts cannot but be the 'whole Christ'. Their charity cannot but take the universal dimensions of the love of Christ, and so they bear the whole divine *plêrôma* which is the Church and the New Creation (cf Eph 3:17-20). Though distinct, the charismatic gifts of virginity and apostolate are linked together by a deep kinship. It is not by chance that the Apostle was a virgin and that the Virgin was the mother of all the faithful.

Conclusion

Christian virginity is a form of fecundity, a higher form since it belongs to the restored order of the eschatological world.

This does not mean that virginity is fecund of its own power. Like the cross, which it recalls and in dependence on which it stands, it would be senseless and would express nothing but the hopelessness of this world, would be mere despair and failure, but for the Spirit and his vivifying power (cf I Cor 15:19).

Virginal fecundity is due to the Spirit. It is he who exerts his power on the virgin's impotent flesh. It is he also who prepares the virgin to be fitting material, ready to lend itself to his action. Virginity is total surrender to the Spirit; the flesh gives way to the divine might and abandons itself to its work, corresponding fully to its impulses and actions.

This is what the authors of the New Testament and Luke particularly intend to describe in Mary. She is poor; she is the handmaid of the Lord. She represents the powerlessness of the flesh. Yet in her the flesh is already cleansed by humility. She is weak but her weakness is rich with faith and hope, as it was with the poor of the Old Testament, as it will be especially in the Servant suffering on the cross. When the Spirit comes down upon her, he will work in her much more than a miracle: the fruit of Mary's womb marks the dawn of salvation. For, born of the Spirit, he is in the flesh the first cell of the new world, the embodiment of the divine power and glory, a man endowed with the privileges of the divine sonship.

The Virgin represents mankind which, by the grace of the Spirit, becomes pregnant with divine life. This reformed mankind lives and spreads in the Church, for in her the life-giving work of the Holy Ghost is carried out and goes on bringing Christ to the world. The Church stands in the world as the sign of the virgin who begets. Like the Virgin, the Church is apparently sterile. She cannot and will not claim worldly efficacy. She will not compete with the powers of the world for might and prestige. She does not create new techniques, will not go in search of new planets and unknown continents. Hers is not to expand man's universe and make it yield more. The outcome of her work is the advent of Christ and, in Christ, of the regenerated world announced by the prophets. The aim of the Church is not the organization and propagation of the present life but its renovation. The life she brings is the divine life, the gift of the Spirit.

Every Christian is thus begotten and in turn may and must become instrumental in making the world share in that new birth. Yet the spiritual fecundity of Mary and of the Church is most fully contained and realized in virginal life.

For what happened in the spotless Mary when the fullness of the Godhead which was in Christ shone out through

her, happens in every soul that leads by rule the virgin life.
No longer indeed does the Master come with bodily
presence; we know Christ no longer according to the
flesh (II Cor 5:16). But spiritually he dwells in us and
brings us his Father along with him, as the Gospel
somewhere tells. Such is the power of virginity that it
dwells in heaven near the Father of Spirits . . . that it
obtains the salvation of mankind and draws down the
Deity to share man's estate.[1]

Such is the charism of virgins. To them it has been given to
conceive the Word and to bear it to the world. Their life
bears witness to the new fecundity which the Spirit initiated
in Mary, fulfilled on the Cross and continues in the Church.
Theirs it is to sing, in their whole life, the joyful song of the
heavenly Jerusalem:

> Rejoice, o barren woman who never bore child;
> break into a shout of joy,
> you who never knew a mother's pangs:
> for the deserted wife shall have more children
> than she who lives with the husband.
> (Is 54:1; Gal 4:27)[2]

---

[1] Gregory of Nyssa, *De Virginitate*, 2, *PG* 46, 324C.
[2] This quotation is given according to the *New English Version*.

Conclusion

Conclusion

FROM JEREMIAS to Jesus and his disciples, and particularly Paul and Luke, we have tried to retrace in these pages the main outlines of the biblical concept of virginity and the main stages of its development.

The Old Testament hardly knew celibacy. Jeremias had perceived to some extent its negative value and had embraced it as a prophecy of the imminent ruin and as the fitting condition of man living in a doomed world. It was Jesus who gave celibacy its positive meaning. By inviting the disciples to practise continence 'in view of the Kingdom', he opened new prospects, showing virginity as the ideal condition of the citizen of God's Kingdom.

It remained to investigate those new prospects. As the first Christian generations saw better the nature of the Kingdom and in proportion to their growing awareness of its requirements, the meaning of virginity was also understood more and more deeply. Seeing better the relation of the Kingdom to the death and resurrection of Christ and its impact in the daily life of the faithful, the Early Church also perceived more and more clearly the latent implications of Jesus' call to virginity 'in view of the Kingdom'.

When studying this development, we moved from the

147

future to the past and to the present. Our starting point was the meaning of virginity as regards the Kingdom to come. From there, we passed to its relation with the paschal sacrifice and its bearing on the present life. We think that this approach was precisely that which was followed by the New Testament. When first uttered by the Master, the call to celibacy had a definite eschatological ring, in accord with the general tone of Jesus' Galilean preaching. Enlightened by the Spirit, the disciples soon perceived the new depth of meaning which the death and resurrection of the Lord had given to his eschatological teaching.

Further investigation of the theological significance of celibacy was the work of the two great theologians of the Christian beginnings, Paul and Luke. Both practised total continence: it is not surprising that they applied their thoughts to the value of the condition they had embraced and that, without distorting the meaning of the Lord's exhortation, they endeavoured to bring out its relevance in the mystery of salvation and to translate it into terms of daily life.

Paul did this mostly in his reply to the query of the Corinthians in I Cor 7. His answer, complete and far-reaching, was our guide in the main stages of our work.

More discreetly, Luke revealed his thoughts in the pages of his Gospel. But his discretion must not deceive us. Either because he owed it to Paul's teaching or because it was the fruit of his own reflexion, his insight makes him Paul's equal as a theologian of virginity. Moreover he showed a deep connaturality of soul with the Virgin Mary. Nobody understood so well as he did the role she played and the place her virginity occupied in the history of salvation.

Finally it can be said that it is Luke's portrait of the Virgin

Mary that constitutes the best synthesis of the biblical doctrine of virginity.

Mary, the mother of the Saviour, is a virgin. Her virginity is 'lowliness', a poverty that turns already towards the cross and has the same significance, augurs the end of the present world and shows a flesh stripped of all conceit.

But already, in Mary's virginity, the paradox of the cross is manifested. By the power of the Spirit, her meanness is changed into glory (cf Phil 2:8f) and death into life. The poor are exalted (Lk 1:52); the virgin gives birth and her fecundity is divine.

Thus Mary's virginity, by a proleptic participation in the cross, announced the end of the world of flesh and the dawn of the new creation revived by the Spirit. By the grace of the Spirit, this mystery is continued and shown forth in the virginal life of the disciples.

But to keep the genuine Christian value, virginity must be lived in the spirit which animated Mary. For virginity is not necessarily a Christian attitude. It is possible to observe perfect continence in a quite un-Christian way.

Continence and virginity may be completely pagan. The Vestals are a well known case of sacral continence in paganism: dedicated to the cult of the deity, they had to preserve their virginity during a minimum of thirty years after their *consecratio*. Sacrificial virginity was also to be found in Greek mythology, which had several stories of virgins offered or offering themselves in sacrifice to placate the gods.[1] The idea behind these myths or the virginal cult

[1] The story of Iphigeneia is well known but it is not the only one. 'Euripides has treated this favourite theme of his in nine tragedies, six of which are still extant and three lost' (G. Herzog-Hauser in Pauly-Wissowa, *Realencyclopädie der Classischen Altertumswissenschaft* XVIII, 2, col. 1909).

of Vesta was that virginity 'stands for the bloom of youthful life and for absolute innocence: in both there abides a religious power . . . Their sacrifice has a special force because they give their life in the freshness of youth and in the state of innocence. They become therefore σώτειραι and they are invoked in case of need.'[1] Thus an inscription on the statue of a Vestal said that 'the state could feel day after day the effects of her chastity and of her exactitude in fulfilling the sacred rites':[2] virginity had a kind of magic or at least a ritual influence on the gods. These beliefs obviously stand against a background of nature worship.

The continence of the few philosophers who considered it as a virtue was immune from beliefs of this kind; but it was not immune from self-sufficiency. It aimed at a perfect control of the soul over the body. It represented a longing for moral greatness, an attempt to free the soul from the weight of the body, to let it soar towards God in pure contemplation. This was a high ideal, but great was the danger of pride in it.

The significance of Mary's virginity is entirely different from both cultic virginity and philosophical continence. Mary knows that her virginity has no value of its own and no power but that of the Spirit. She does not speak of the greatness of her virginity. For her, it is not virginity that makes her great: it is the Lord (Lk 1:49). As far as she is concerned, she is nothing and her virginity seals her nothingness. Because she is a virgin, she is 'poor', a contemptible thing, considered worthless by the world. Of course, in the case of Mary as in that of the 'Poor of Yahweh' in the Old

[1] G. Delling in *TWNT* V, p. 826.
[2] Quoted in Pauly-Wissowa, *Realencyclopädie* . . ., XVI, 2, col. 1737, which quotes also another text: *redimunt vitam populi procerumque salutem.*

Testament, poverty should be taken in the biblical sense. It is not merely negative. It does not mean only destitution. As we find it in the life of the great biblical figures such as Jeremias, Job, the *Anawim* in the Psalms and the Suffering Servant in Is 52-53, poverty is a religious attitude which underlies the spiritual development of the Old Testament and prepares the way for the abasement of the cross, the imprint of which it bears by anticipation. Biblical poverty does indeed mean life deprived of any human hope but also and mostly 'at its deepest, "radical detachment" (Regamey), total humility and consequently utter confidence in God'.[1] Mary's virginity belongs to this type of poverty. It is a form of that religious attitude made up of 'faith and abandon, joy and confidence; it is akin to humility and can be summarized as an attitude of religious expectation . . . It is silence, readiness, emptiness'.[2] And her greatness comes from the faith and confidence in God which spring in the heart of that emptiness, and from the answer God gave to that faith and confidence.

Virginity of this kind differs entirely from its pagan counterparts. It does not represent an attempt to substitute man's influence for God's power: on the contrary, Mary has no other ambition than to be the handmaid of the Lord. Neither does Mary's virginity correspond to a merely human longing for purity and moral greatness. Her virginity does not belong so much to the moral as to the theological virtues. It manifests an attitude before God rather than an effort of moral perfection and of self-achievement. Luke's Gospel of the Infancy does not describe in Mary a heroic form of the virtue of chastity. What it sees in her is sheer faith

---

[1] A. Gelin, *Les Pauvres de Yahvé*, Paris 1953, p. 154.
[2] *Ibid.*, p. 153.

and hope which has no reliance in creatures but is entirely turned towards God.

Christian celibacy must follow the pattern set by Mary. It must not be pagan. This is not so remote a temptation as it may seem: it is still possible nowadays to be continent in a pagan way like the Vestals, or at least to let pagan infiltrations enter a dedicated life. It happens when one gives way to a spiritual pride that attributes to virginity an efficacy of its own by virtue of its moral greatness. In the measure in which virginity is paraded as a proof of self-control and gives way to superiority complex and self confidence, it is no longer Christian. And it is sheer paganism if it represents a Pelagian attempt to influence God by the force of man's moral achievements and to bring salvation by virtue. If man takes pride in his 'purity' and relies on his moral strength to reach heaven, he is still a pagan; he has not yet known God's mercy and might.

Again, to be fully Christian, the virginity of the disciple must not be mere philosophical continence. Like that of Mary, it must go beyond moral virtue to represent a theological attitude of complete surrender to God. Christian virginity must not be merely 'virtuous'. It is obvious that moral fortitude is necessary to preserve virginity, but a virginity that remains at the level of moral virtue would not be truly Christian; it would not be part of the new life in Christ. It might have a human beauty; it would not be a participation in the κένωσις of the cross and would not be shaped on the ταπείνωσις of Mary. Christian virginity must aim at a total identification with the crucified Lord: it must mean total dispossession of self and be woven of pure faith and love.

Humility will be the proof that virginity is truly Christian.

If it is really rooted in a theological attitude of surrender to God, virginity will be humble because it will be lost in God. Like Mary, the Christian who has embraced dedicated celibacy will be humble not only because he will be conscious that his continence is the fruit of God's grace but also because he will know that his virtue consists precisely in his having none, and that the state he lives in has no other value than that given it by the Spirit.

And if he has great virtue . . ., there is still much wanting to him: . . . that having left all things else, he leave also himself and wholly go out of himself and retain nothing of self-love. And when he shall have done all things which he knows should be done, let him think that he has done nothing. Let him not take great account of that which may appear much to be esteemed, but let him in truth acknowledge himself to be an unprofitable servant: as Truth itself has said: When you shall have done all these things which are commanded you, say, We are unprofitable servants (Lk 17:10). Then he may be truly poor in spirit, and may say with the prophet, I am alone and poor (Ps 25:16). Yet no one is indeed richer than such a man, none more powerful, none more free.[1]

There is no other real Christian virginity than that which has given up every form of human glory, fecundity and influence. For then it is God's might that raises the virgins from their lowliness and God's joy that fills them in their loneliness.

---

[1] *Imit. Christi*, II, xi, 4f.

11

General Index

Main references are given in italic numerals

Aaron, 76
Abraham, 77, 111, 134
Achimelek, 71
Adam, 126, 133
    New Adam, 70, 119f, 135, 139
Ad Catholici Sacerdotii, 77
Agapê, 97f, 103, *105-109* (see Charity, Love)
Albigenses, 90
ALLEN, W. C., 115n
ALLO, 30, 58n
'*almah*, 137
'*anawim*, 62, 151 (see Poverty)
Angels, 45f, 84
Anthropology (supernatural), 88, 133
Apocalyptic literature, 31, 41f
Apostolate, 140f
Apotheosis, 86
Ark of Covenant, 73f
Ascension, 112 (see Glorification, Exaltation, Resurrection)
Âshrama, 90
Ataraxia, 91, 100
Atonement (Day of), 76
AUDET, J. P., 114n
AUGUSTINE, St, 25n

Baptism, 96
BARRETT, C. K., 86, 116, 117n
BAUMGARTER, 91n
Beatitudes, 105

BENOIT, P., 127n
BERNARD, St, 110
Birth-control, 95
Birth pains, 34, 70, 137ff, 143
Bodmer Papyrus, 130
Body, 46, 66f, 69, 71, 81, 83, 90, 93, 109, 150
    of Christ (Church), 68, 99, 103, 105, 107, 120
BOISMARD, M. E., 118n, 130, 131n
BOSSUET, 25
BOUYER, L., 48n, 88
BOVER, P., 126n
BRAUN, F. M., 66n, 130n
Bride, Bridegroom, (see Matrimony)
Buddhism, xiv, 90
BULTMANN, R., 55n, 63, 116

CALES, J., 32n
CALLAN, 30, 58n
Calvary, see Cross
CALVIN, 85n
CAMBIER, J., 47n, 137n
CAMELOT, P. T., 80n
CAMELOT, TH., 48n
CARCOPINO, J., 95n
Carrying the Cross, 61-67
Cathari, 90
Celibacy, of Apostles, 57
    Buddhist, 90

155

Celibacy—continued
of Elias, 25
among Essenes, 20ff, 71
according to the Fathers, 48, 70,
80, 82, 84, 99f, 110ff
heretical views on —, 90
Hindu, 57, 90
in the Hellenistic World, 89ff,
150
of Jeremias, 25-30
of Jesus, 38, 40, 43, 48
of John the Baptist, 21, 40
of Luke, 60, 148
neo-platonic, 90f
of Paul, 60, 148
Protestant views on —, xvi, 85
selfish, viii, 89, 95
and Stoicism, 89, 91
(*see* Continence, Virginity)
Celsus, 104
CERFAUX, L., 33, 47n, 68, 99n,
137n
Charisma, xvi, 35, 43, 48, 69, 85,
91, 113, 140f
Charity, 46, 91, 97, 99, *101-110*
(*see* *Agapê*, Love)
Chastity, xv, 114, 151 (*see* Moral
value of continence)
Child, 44f, 139
Church, 68, 88, 103, 105f, 108, 111,
134-140, 141ff
CICERO, 77
Circumcision, 67
Cleanness, 71-74
CLEMENT OF ALEXANDRIA, 130n
COHEN, R., 95n
Conjugal harmony, 96f
love, 46, 95, *105*ff
relations, 71ff, 76f, 81
Consecration, 76, 81f, 85f, 109, 150
Continence of Aaron, 76
of High Priest, 76
in Israel, 19-22, 72-78
Rabbinical Views on, 20, 77f
on Sabbath Day, 77f
(*see* Celibacy, Virginity)

CORNELY, 30
Covenant (new), 37, 41, 83
(old), 28, 36, 72
CRAWLEY, A. E., 95n
Creation (and the Spirit), 115-121
Cross, 29, 33, 35, 37, 47, 51, *61-70*,
86, 88, 91, 105, 107f, 121ff,
125, 135, 138, 140f, 143, 147ff,
151
CULLMANN, O., 33, 42, 43, 46, 135
Cult, of the New Testament, 78-86
of the Old Testament, 72-78, 82f
CYPRIAN, 48

Daily death, 66-69, 139
life, 64f, *69*, 75, 143
DALMAN, G., 41n
Damascus Document, 22
DAVEY, F. N., 133n, 136n
David, 71, 120, 126
Day of the Lord, 28, 36
of the Messias, 77
Death, *26-29*, 35, 46, 92f, 133,
139, 149
of Christ, *see* Cross
Dedication, 82, 85, 102f, 105
Defilement, 67, *71-74*, 81 (*see*
Cleanness)
DELLING, G., 103n, 150n
Descendants, 67, 139
Desert, 99, 101, 137
Discipleship, 54, 59-61, 64
Divorce, 38, 44
DODD, C. H., 42
Donatists, 90
Dualism (Greek), 90, 92, 100
DUBARLE, A.-M., 136n
DUPLACY, J., 130n
DUPONT, A.-Sommer, 22n
DUPONT, J., 40n, 44, 56, 59-60
Dura-Europos, 117
DURRWELL, X., 83n

Ebionism, 56
Elias, 25
Encratists, 59, 67, 90

End of the World, 25-36, 147
EPICTECTUS, 89, 90
Eschatology ('consequent'), 31, 42 ('realized'), 42
(*see* End of the World, Resurrection)
Essenes, 20-22, 71, 117
Eucharist, xiv, 66
Eunuchs, xv, 38f, 61f
Euripides, 149
Exaltation, 83, 85f, (*see* Resurrection, Glorification)
Exodus, 28, *93*, 96, 99, *101*, 111f

Faith, 34, 66, 139ff, 151
Family, 54f, 57, 64
Fatherhood of God, 133, 140, 143 of the Apostle, 140f
Fecundity, 20, 29, 34f, 104, 113, *125-143*
FEUILLET, A., 110n, 136n, 137
Flesh, 29f, 37, 46, 66f, 69, 91-94, 101, 106, 108, 120f, 123, 125, 129-133, 138, 140ff, 149
Foeticide, 95
Form Criticism, 40
FOERSTER, W., 94n, 117n
Furciferi, 64

GELIN, A., 102
Glorification, 109, 129 (*see* Exaltation, Resurrection)
Glory, 68, 75, 81, 85f, 93, 99f, 115, 121-125, 129, 132
Gnosticism, 90
GREGORY OF NYSSA, 48, 84, 143n
GRELOT, P., 77n

Heaven, 41, 84
Heavenly liturgy, 82-84
Hellenism, 89-91, 116
Hermetism, 86
HERZOG-HAUSER, G., 149n
Hieros Gamos, 104, 116
Hinduism, 57, 90
hol, 73f (see Profane)

Holocaust, 82f, 85, 108f (*see* Sacrifice)
Holy, *71-86*, 88, 105, 119
Holy of Holies, 83 (*see* Temple)
Holy Land, 77, 100f
HOSKYNS, E., 136n
Hour, 139 (see καιρός)
HOUSSIAU, A., 130n, 133n, 134n
HUBY, J., 32
Humility, 44, 141, *151-153* (*see* Poverty)

IGNATIUS OF ANTIOCH, 130n
Immolation, 82f, 85f (*see* Sacrifice)
IMSCHOOT, P. VAN, 74n
Incarnation, 109, 119f, 126, 128, 133f
Infancy Gospel, 104, 113-134
IRENEUS, 115n, 130n, 133n
Iphigeneia, 149
Isaac, 63, 134
ISIDORUS OF PELUSIA, 29

Jealousy, 102f
Jephte's daughter, 19f, 27
Jeremias, 22, 25-30, 35, 37, 151
Jerusalem, 35, 37, 113, 122 (*see* Temple, Land of Promise)
Job, 151
John the Baptist, 21, 40
JOHN OF THE CROSS, 110
JOSEPHUS, 21, 57n
JUSTIN, 130n, 134n

keli, 71
Kingdom of God, *38-48*, 62f, 68, 93, 98f, 113, 147
Kingship, 28, 35
KNABENBAUER, J., 126n
KÖHLER, L., 20
KRAELING, C. H., 117n
KÜMMEL, W. G., 42, 43

LAGRANGE, M.-J., 54n, 56, 60n, 64, 115n, 128

LAURENTIN, R., 21n, 115n, 122n, 127n
Law, 72, 79
LEMONNIER, 30
LÉON-DUFOUR, X., 102
Liberty, 89-100
Life, 64, 92, 139
  (divine), 86, 132f, 142
  (new), 41, 68f, 88, 98, *118*, 122 (*see* καινὴ κτίσις, New World)
LIGHTFOOT, R. H., 136n, 139n
Liturgy, 81, 85 (*see* Cult, Heavenly Liturgy)
LOISY, A., 63n, 65n
Loneliness, 26, 29, 74f, 153
Love, 35, 83, 86, 94, 97, 100, 105 (*see Agapê*, Charity, Conjugal Love)
Luke, celibacy of, 60, 148
  contacts with John, 65, 130
  contacts with Paul, 65ff, 123, 128, 148
  radicalism of, 56, 59f
  use of sources, 53-68, 120
LYONNET, S., 127

Malthusianism, 95
Manicheism, xvi
Martyrdom, 47
Mary (fecundity of), 113-143, (*see* Virginity)
Matrimony, profane, 29, 31, 35, 38, 44ff, 57, 66, 77, 78-81, 90, *93-98*, *105-109*
  spiritual, (God with Israel), 27, 103f
  (Christ and the Church), 35, 46, *103*, 105f, 108f, 137
  (of Virgins), 102-113
MCALLAN, W. C., 54n
Mesha Stone, 20
MÉDEBIELLE, A., 126n, 127n
MERK, 54n
Messianic woes, 34
METHODIUS, 70, 110f

Michelangelo, 100
Midrash, 32, 79
Mishna, 76
Missionary, 43, 91
MOLLAT, D., 66n, 130n
Moral value of continence, 80, 114, *150ff*
Mortification, 76, 140 (*see* Renouncement, νέκρωσις)
Moses, 75, 100
Motherhood, 20 (*see* Fecundity)
MUNSTER, L., 108n
Mysteries (pagan), 104
Mystery (marriage as a), 104-108

NATHAN, RABBI, 77, 78
Neofiti Targum, 117
Neoplatonism, 90f
New World, 34, 37, 40, 48, 68, 70, 93, 99f, 113, 115, *117-121*, 125, 133ff, 141f, 149 (*see* καινὴ κτίσις, Kingdom)

OEPKE, A., 90n
'*olah*, 83 (*see* Holocaust)
Old Man, 66, 70
OLIER, M., 86
Once for all, 85, 135
'*oni*, 124 (*see* ταπείνωσις, Poverty)
ORIGEN, 40n, 54, 82n, 110, 115n, 130
OSTY, 30, 58n, 61, 120n, 122n
OTTO, R., 74n

Pagan celibacy, 95, *149-152*
Paschal symbolism, 122f
Parousia, 32-34, 37, 103, 105
PAULY-WISSOWA, 149n, 150n
PEDERSEN, J., 20n, 42n, 73n, 131n
Pelagianism, xvi, 152
Phidias, 100
PHILO, 80n
Platonism, 90, 100, 109
Please, desire to, 88, 94-99, 101f
PLINY, 21
PLUMMER, A., 31n, 59, 60, 65n, 89

PODECHARD, E., 78n
POLYBIUS, 95n
Poverty, 44f, 62, 96, 123ff, 134, 141, *149ff*, 153
Power, 42, 45, 93, 99, 109, 119ff, *125*, 129, 141, 151
PRAT, 32, 33, 58n
Priesthood of Christ, 82ff
Private Property, 59
PROCKSCH, O., 74n
Procreation, 35, 43, 46, 66, 75, 77 (*see* Fecundity)
(Duty of), 29, 57, 75, 90
Profane, 73-78, 81
Proleptic Deliverance of the Body, the, 46
Promise and Fulfilment, 42
PSEUDO DEMOSTHENES, 96n
PSEUDO JEROME, 130n
Purity, *see* Chastity, Cleanness, Moral Value of Continence

qâdôsh, 73, 80f (*see* Holy)
QUASTEN, E. J., 111n
Qumran, *see* Essenes

raḥam, 20
Renouncement, 55f, 60, *61-70*, 132 (*see* Cross, νέκρωσις)
Rest, *see* Sabbath
Resurrection, of Christ, 33, 66, *85f*, 88, 99, 112, *118-121*, 125, 128f, 137, 147f (*see* Glory, Ascension, Exaltation)
of Men, 28, 33, 37, 40, 45f, 48, 111, *117f*
REES, W., 30, 58n
RENAN, 56
RICCIOTTI, G., 58n
ROBERT, A., 108n, 110n
ROBERTSON, A., 31n, 89
ruaḥ, 116, 117 (*see* Spirit)

Sabbath, 77f
Sacra Virginitas, 108

Sacraments, 43, 46, 66, 81, 97f 106f, 135, 139
Sacrifice, *82-86*, 105ff, 108, 148
Sara, 134
Sanctuary, *see* Temple
Samnyâsi, 57, 90
SCHLATTER, A., 64n
SCHMIDT, 40n
SCHNEIDER, 40n
SCHWEITZER, A., 31, 42
SCHWEIZER, E., 117n
shâkan, 115
shekinah, 78, 81, 115, 127
sheol, 29
Signs, 34, *42f*, 48, 68, *105-108*, 13f 138, 140
Sin, 21, 92f
Sinai, 72, 75, 79, 82
SJOBERG, 117n
SOCRATES, 80
Sonship (divine), 119, *126-134*, 142
SPICQ, C., 32, 58n
Spirit, 29f, 37, 41ff, 46, 48f, 66, 68ff, 79, 84, 92f, 104f, 106, 109, *113-121*, 123-129, *132ff*, 135, 140ff, 149f, 153
Spirit (and matter), 45, 90-93
STEINMANN, J., 70n
Sterility, 20, 124f, 135, 142
Stoicism, 21, 89, 91, 150
Sublimation, 83
Suffering Servant, 142, 151
Symbolism, 27, 47, 107, 136
Symposium on chastity, 110

TAYLOR, V., 63
tâhôr, 73 (*see* Cleanness)
tâmê', 73 (*see* Defilement)
Temperance, 114
Temple, 28, 35, 73, 76f, 81, 83, 115, 122, 127f, 132
TERTULLIAN, 130n
Things of the Lord, 99f
THURIAN, M., xvi, 85n
TOYNBEE, A. J., 95n

Union with Christ, 63, *66-70*, 109,
     (*see* Carrying the Cross, Dis-
     cipleship, Resurrection)
Urias, 71

Vaganay, L., 38, 39n, 55n
Vaux, R. de, 71n, 73n, 74n, 83n
Vermes, G., 22n
Vestals, 149, 152
Virgin Birth, *see* Fecundity
Virginity, of Jephte's daughter,
     19f, 27
   of Mary, 20f, 48, 62, 103, *148-
     153*
   of the Vestals, 150f
Vow of virginity, 85
   of Mary, 21

War (eschatological), 21, 55, 64,
     69, 71
   (sacred), 71-73
*War of the Children of Light against
   the Children of Darkness*, 21, 71f

Weakness, 123ff, 133ff, 141f
Wealth, 96
Widows, xv, 40, 60
Wisdom, 117
Woman, in Hellenism, 95, 96
   in Israel, *19f*, 124, 131
Woodhouse, W. J., 95n
Word of God, xvi, 98, 131, 143
   personified in Christ, 79, 128,
     131, 135
Work, 77
   good —, xvi
World, 30, 35, 49, 69, 86, 88, *91-
   94*, 100f, 108
Worries (apostolic), 91f, 99f
   (worldly), 89, 96, 98, 112
Wrath of God, 36, 100

Xenophon, 80n

Zealots, 64

Index of Scripture References

Genesis

1:2	115, 116, 117n
1:4	29
1:10	29
1:28	29, 67, 77, 90
2:4	115
2:24	57
8:1	117
12:1	112

Exodus

19:14	72
20:8-11	77
40:35	115

Leviticus

8:33	76
9:24	83
22:2-7	71n

Numbers

10:35	73
21:14	73

Deuteronomy

11:10-17	77n
22:9	73
23:10-15	73
25:5-10	131

Josue

7:13	73
13:14	75
13:33	75
14:3	75
18:7	75

Judges

4:14	73
5:30	20
11:37-40	19

I Samuel

1:11	124
2:1	124
2:5	124
2:7	124
4	73
18:17	73
21:4-6	71, 74
25:28	73

II Samuel

5:24	73
11:4	73
11:8-13	71
14:7	131

IV Kings (Septuagint)

18:14	65

II Chronicles

7:1	83

Job

1:5	73
5:6	92n
21:3	65
27:3	116
32:8	116
33:4	116

Psalms
25:16   153
33:6   116
45   111
73:25-28   78
104:30   116, 117
113   123
127:3-5   20
147:18   116

Proverbs
8:22   116

Canticle
8:6   108

Wisdom
7:22-27   117
18:13   128

Isaias
7:14   138
13:3   73
20:1-6   27
26:16   139
41:17   93
43:18f   115
43:19   93
44:3   116
51:6   93
52-53   151
52:11   93
54:1   143
54:5f   103
62:5   103
65:17-20   93
66:7   138, 139
66:22   93
67:17   115

Jeremias
3:1   103
4:23-31   28
9:19-21   27
11:19-23   28
12:6   28

Jeremias—continued
15:2-4   28
15:17   29
16:1-4   26
16:9   29
19:1-11   27
20:2   28
20:8   27
22:7   73
31:15   28
31:31-35   30, 37
36:5   28
36:26   28
51:27f   73

Lamentations
1:15   20
2:13   20

Ezechiel
4:1-5:4   27
8:1-11:25   28
16:6-43   103
23:38   73
37   118
37:1-14   28, 93, 116

Daniel
7:27   41n

Osee
1-3   27
2:21f   103

Joel
1:8   20, 103, 138
1:14   76
2:15   76
2:16   75

Amos
5:2   20, 138

Michaeas
7:6   55

Matthew		Luke—continued	
1:1	114, 115	1:26	122
1:18	114, 115, 120	1:25	19, 124
5:3	44	1:32	120, 123
5:32	39, 57	1:34	21, 114
6:10	42	1:35	115, 119, 120, 123, 127, 128, 130, 132
10:37	54		
10:38	64, 65	1:35b	126
11:27	128	1:43	123
12:28	42	1:46	124
16:24	63, 64	1:48	20, 62, 124
19:3-12	44	1:49	150
19:5	57	1:51	124
19:6	57	1:52	124, 129
19:9	39, 57	1:53	124
19:10-12	38	2	122f
19:10-26	44	2:32	122
19:11	43	2:34	122
19:12	22, 38, 43, 61, 62	2:39	122
19:16-26	44	2:42	122
19:27	57	2:49	122
19:29	53	5:11	56n, 57
19:30	45	5:28	56n, 57
20:16	45	8:3	59
22:30	45		
24:9-28	31		
25:1-13	111	8:14	96
		9:23	63, 65
Mark		10:22	128
4	42	10:38-42	59
4:10	39	12:33	56n
4:34	39	14:20	58
7:17	39	14:26	53, 54, 58, 59, 62
8:34	62, 64, 65	14:27	65
9:30	39	14:33	56, 59
10:7	57	15	44
10:9	57	16:1-9	44
10:10-12	39	16:18	39, 57
10:11	57	17:10	153
10:28	57	17:21	42
10:29	53	18:22	56n
10:32	39	18:24	62
12:25	79n	18:29	53, 56, 58, 62
		20:35	46
Luke		21:23	31
1	22, 122f		

John

1:12f	129
1:13	130, 132
1:14	79, 115, 132
2:1	131
2:1-11	135
2:3	131
2:5	131
2:12	131
3:3	133
3:6	132
3:14	37
3:31	132
6:26-40	98
6:53-63	132
7:38f	135
8:33-38	132
8:53-58	132
16	140
16:19-22	137
16:20	139
17:15	86
17:19	86
17:23	86
17:24	86
17:26	86
19:17	65
19:25	131, 135
19:34-37	135

Acts

2:16ff	33
2:36	129
2:44f	56n, 59
3:15	121
4:32	56n, 59
4:34	56n, 59
5:4	60
6:1	59
9:19	59
11:26	59
13:33	137

Romans

1:3f	119, 120, 128
1:4	128

Romans—continued

4:13-17	134
5:5	109
6:3-6	66
6:7-11	66
7:4	66
8	118
8:5-13	66
8:9	140
8:11	118
8:14	118
8:20f	94
8:23	120
8:29	118
9:6-12	134
12:1	82
13:11	31
14:14	67
14:20	67
16:1	58n

I Corinthians

1:23	125
1:25	125
1:27f	125
3:17	80
4:14	140
6:15-20	81
6:19	81
6:20	81
7	22, 40n, 71, 80, 88, 91, 93, 97, 98, 102n, 104, 148
7:1	60
7:5	57
7:7	35, 60
7:8	40n
7:10	58
7:15	58n
7:17	58
7:25	61
7:26	30, 33
7:26-31	32
7:27	58
7:28	31
7:29	31

I Corinthians—continued

7:29-31	30
7:32	81, 101
7:32-35	30, 33, 88
7:33	94
7:34	72, 79, 80, 81, 82
7:35	112
9:5	57
9:19	100
9:22	94
10:1-11	93
10:4	32
10:33	94n
11:2-16	32
13:12	107
15:19	141
15:44-50	118
15:45-49	109

II Corinthians

1:22	120
4:5-6	x
4:9	66
4:10-12	66
5:5	120
5:16	143
5:17	118
6:13	140
6:16	81, 118
11:2	46, 102, 104, 105
11:23-27	91
11:29	92
12:1-10	91

Galatians

1:10	98
2:19	66
4:3	93
4:4	131
4:19	140
4:22-31	134
4:26f	134
4:27	143
6:15	118

Ephesians

2:15	118

Ephesians—continued

2:21	81
3:17	140
3:17-20	141
4:24	118
5:25-33	35, 80, 90, 104-6
5:29	46

Philippians

1:21	140
2:5-9	129
2:7	121, 125
2:8	149
3:20	101

Colossians

1:18	34
1:24	34
2:11	67
3:1-3	101

I Thessalonians

2:8	140
2:11	140
3:7	31
4:8	118

II Thessalonians

1:6	31

I Timothy

5:3-5	40n

Philemon

2	58n
10	140

Hebrews

1:5	137
1:6	118
2:1-4	93
3:1-3	93
5:5	137
7:27	84
9:7-12	84
9:9	31
9:12	84
9:14	82, 84, 85

Hebrews—continued

10:10	84
10:12	84
12:18-22	82
12:28	82
12:29	85

I Peter

1:5	31
1:11	31
2:11	93

II Peter

3:8	34

I John

2:17	34
2:18	33

Apocalypse

1:5	118, 137
1:9	31

Apocalypse—continued

7	47
7:14	31, 47
11:11	118
12	136, 138, 140
12:1-5	137
12:2	136
12:5	136
12:6	137
12:11	138
12:13-17	137
12:17	136
14	47
14:1-5	46
14:4	138
15:1-5	93
20:4	118
21	37
21:3	118
22:17	135

Index of Greek Words

Main references are given in italics

ἄγαμος xv
ἀγάπη 97f, 103, *105-109* (*see* Charity, Love)
ἅγιος 8of, 82 (*see* Holy)
ἀγὼν 69
ἀδελφή 57f
αἴρειν 65
ἀμέριμνος 89
ἀνάγκη 3of
ἀρέσκειν 94
ἀταραξία 91

βαστάζειν 65

γένεσις 114f, 120
γέννησις 115

διά 41
διὸ καί 126f
δύναμις 121 (*see* Power)

ἐγκρατής xv
ἔκστασις 91, 93
ἐπισκιάζειν 115, 127

θλῖψις 31, 34

ἱερὸς γάμος 104

καθ' ἡμέραν 64

καινὴ κτίσις 118-121 (*see* New World)
καιρός 31, 123
κενοῦν 121
κένωσις 121, 152
κύριος 99f

λαμβάνειν 65

μισεῖν 55, 58

νέκρωσις 66f, 85
νοῦς 92

ὀλιγανθρωπία 95
ὄνειδος 124

πάθημα 34
παρθένος xv, 137
πλήρωμα 141
πνεῦμα *see* Spirit
πνεῦμα ζωοποιοῦν 120f

σώτειρα 150

ταπεινοῦν 126
ταπείνωσις 20, 62, *124f*, 152 (*see* Poverty)

ὕλη 92

Barre, Vt., 05641

DATE BORROWED